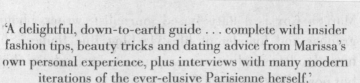
Practising Pa...

'A delightful, down-to-earth guide . . . complete with insider fashion tips, beauty tricks and dating advice from Marissa's own personal experience, plus interviews with many modern iterations of the ever-elusive Parisienne herself.'

Monica de La Villardière, writer and presenter for Elle.fr & British Vogue, *and Co-founder of the* Fashion No Filter *podcast*

'*Practising Parisienne* is a celebration of the City of Lights and an ode to the pleasures in life. Marissa Cox effortlessly mixes practical tips, personal stories and inspiring conversations in this charming guide to living well the Parisian way.'

Miranda York, author of At the Table *and* The Food Almanac

'It's taken a very observant and open-minded infiltrator to truly crack the mysterious code to French allure. With appreciation, honesty, a deep understanding and access to leading figures, *Practising Parisienne* reads like a who's who and what's what when it comes to everything Parisian.'

Hannah Almassi, Editor in Chief, Who What Wear UK

'Marissa's fresh and realistic guide to life in Paris is peppered with helpful tips and interviews with French taste-makers. Even if you don't find yourself booking a one-way Eurostar ticket to the capital like Marissa, this book might just be the key to finally nailing that elusive Parisian *je ne sais quoi.*'

Penny Goldstone, Fashion Editor, Marie Claire

Marissa Cox is a Paris-based journalist, writer, photographer and founder of lifestyle blog Rue Rodier. She moved to Paris eight years ago, initially for a relationship, but now calls the City of Lights home.

Marissa is a regular contributor for *Who What Wear* UK, where she writes about Parisian style, interiors and skincare. She has written for *Marie Claire* UK, *Cereal*, *Domino magazine* and *Apartment Therapy*. She has been mentioned in *Elle Décor* US, *Time Out*, *Le Figaro*, *EasyJet Traveller*, *Glamour* UK and *Condé Nast Traveler*. Her collaborations include Goutal Paris, Made.com, Le Bon Marché, Citizens of Humanity, Elizabeth Arden, Omega, Galeries Lafayette, Maison Chaumet, Sisley, Gant, Marks & Spencer, GAP, Georgio Armani Beauty, Sézane and KitchenAid.

www.ruerodier.com

Marissa Cox

Practising Parisienne

Lifestyle Secrets from the City of Lights

First published in 2021
by HEADLINE HOME
an imprint of HEADLINE PUBLISHING GROUP

First published in paperback in 2022 by
HEADLINE PUBLISHING GROUP

1

Cataloguing in Publication Data is available from the British Library

ISBN: 978 1 4722 7764 0
eISBN: 978 1 4722 7765 7

Commissioning Editor: Anna Steadman
Senior Editor: Kate Miles
Copy Editor: Tara O'Sullivan
Proofreader: Nikki Sinclair
Indexer: Caroline Wilding
Designed and typeset by EM&EN

Printed and bound in Great Britain by Clays Ltd, Elcograf S.p.A.

MIX
Paper from
responsible sources
FSC® C104740

Headline's policy is to use papers that are natural, renewable and recyclable
products and made from wood grown in well-managed forests and other
controlled sources. The logging and manufacturing processes are expected to
conform to the environmental regulations of the country of origin.

HEADLINE PUBLISHING GROUP
An Hachette UK Company
Carmelite House
50 Victoria Embankment
London
EC4Y 0DZ

www.headline.co.uk
www.hachette.co.uk

For my mum and dad,
whose experiences living abroad and
interest in many of the subjects explored here
inspired me and gave me the courage
to move to Paris and, ultimately,
to write this book

Contents

My Parisienne story

Parisien(ne)
= belonging or relating to Paris

'Être parisien, ce n'est pas être né à Paris,
c'est y renaître'

'To be Parisian is not to be born in Paris,
it is to be reborn there'

Sacha Guitry

It wasn't my lifelong dream to live in Paris. In fact, I never even gave it a thought. Unlike others who have entertained fantasises of *'la vie Parisienne'* they'd borrowed from films like *Amélie, Sabrina, An American in Paris* and *French Kiss,* or from books by Hemingway, Proust and George Orwell, I never imagined myself moving to the City of Lights in search of freshly baked baguettes or buttery croissants. I didn't conjure up romantic notions of sitting on a Parisian terrace with a *café crème,* or of strolling along the quaint streets of Le Marais hand in hand with a French lover; nor did I have visions of admiring the city's rooftops from the Sacré-Coeur. Growing up, Paris wasn't somewhere I aspired to live. In my mind, it remained entirely a place to visit for a romantic weekend with a boyfriend: a destination for discovering art and sipping red wine; somewhere to sample *escargot* and to escape everyday life, but not to make a home. I was more interested in the bright lights of a more modern city. As a teenager, I fantasized about being like Carrie Bradshaw, pounding New York's pavements in a pair of Louboutins and an array of eccentric outfits by day and tapping away on a laptop by night, not Audrey Hepburn in her rather restrained (yet undoubtedly chic) beige trench and flat black ballerinas shouting 'Bonjour, Paris!' from the side of the Seine in *Funny Face*. I dreamed of moving Stateside, of skyscrapers and neon lights. I wanted to drink Manhattan cocktails, and I wanted my money where I could see it: 'hanging in my closet'. I craved modernity and a fast-paced life fuelled by newness, commerce, change and colour. Paris, despite its evident beauty, seemed more like a museum than a bustling, forward-thinking capital city. Don't get me wrong – I didn't dislike Paris. I just never saw living there as part of my *grand plan*.

Truth be told, I never really had a plan. And yet my relationship with France had started when I was a child. Growing up, my family holidayed in France pretty regularly. Every year (or so I seem to recall), from around the age of three, we would take the ferry or hovercraft from Dover or Folkestone and stay in a *gîte* (holiday cottage) in some different part of rural France. Sometimes Brittany, sometimes the Dordogne, sometimes France's Basque Country. Exploring a different area with my parents each year meant that France formed a large part of my growing up. One of the earliest photos of me was taken near the French–Spanish border, with the rolling  green hills of the Pyrenees clearly visible in the background. I'm holding a toy camera (perhaps a hint about my future life working with photography in Paris) and wearing a white pinafore dress with pear shapes stitched to the front. In another, I'm wearing a turquoise-and-white striped dress with a white apron, posing beneath a huge sign advertising Pouilly-Fuissé wine (now, incidentally, one of my favourite appellations – see page 259). At the age of seven, I remember having my likeness drawn in charcoal by a street artist in Saint-Jean-de-Luz – the drawing still hangs on the wall in my dad's apartment in Deal. I remember running screaming from what appeared, to my three-year-old stature, to be tidal waves in Biarritz, imploring my parents to picnic as close to the promenade as possible, as I was petrified of the wild sea. I also remember my mum getting the most horrific food poisoning of her life from an oyster in a restaurant in Brittany one Easter. She was horribly sick for a week, and as a result, I didn't try oysters until I was twenty-three years old. (Today, I love nothing more than a plate of oysters and *un verre* of Muscadet wine bought from le Marché Bastille on a Sunday). And, ironically, I also used to fantasise about getting married in a château surrounded by vineyards (actually, I still do). Oh, and my great-grandfather on my mother's side was French. Apparently I have his eyes. Perhaps I was destined to live in France, after all.

Paris is always a good idea

'A walk about Paris will provide lessons in history, beauty, and in the point of life'
Thomas Jefferson

After a four-year course in English Literature and Hispanic Studies at the University of London, I found myself working in the world of publishing – mainly because I loved books, magazines and reading and I couldn't afford to continue with unpaid internships in journalism. I ended up working in the publicity department for a well-known publisher, but the job never felt quite *right*. All the while, I had this niggling feeling that there was something else out there for me. I wanted to write my own story, not publicise those of others. I craved adventure, and didn't see myself climbing up the ranks of the company.

Perhaps unsurprisingly (because so many stories start this way), my interest in French culture began with a man. One of the most beautiful men I have ever briefly dated. Tall, with blue eyes, a sexy French accent, great style, and dark, wavy hair that made me swoon every time he brushed it away from his face. We met at a friend's house party while I was living in Dalston, East London, and I couldn't take my eyes off him. He dabbled in fashion, but to this day, I have no real idea what he did for a living, other than starting some club night in East London. But I didn't care, and found his French *laissez-faire* and easy attitude towards life so very cool. I probably would have moved to France with him there and then, given the chance, but instead he ghosted me (before ghosting was even really a thing). Either way, that encounter sparked something inside me.

In 2012, I started dating a Portuguese man who lived, as you might have guessed, in Paris. He had moved there for work after stints in London and Brussels. (Part of me now wonders whether it was him or Paris that was the real attraction) We had met through a mutual friend around eight years earlier, when I was in my second year at university in London, and we'd gone on to have a few drunken encounters four or five years later, the final one being when we were deliberately placed next to each other at said friend's wedding in Porto. I was dating someone else at the time, but when that relationship ended, I accepted an invitation to visit him in Paris. The previous year, I had visited LA, and was almost dead-set on moving to California – but that final encounter with my Portuguese love interest steered my ship in a different direction. Admittedly, I was looking for a serious relationship, as well as a change of scenery after seven years living in London – but I never thought that change of scenery would include the Eiffel Tower and learning a new language.

Now, once a month, I found myself staying in his apartment on Rue Rodier in the 9th arrondissement, where we spent weekends hanging out in cafés, enjoying *apéros* at his friends' apartments and exploring Parisian neighbourhoods. I took the 5 a.m. 'red-eye' Eurostar back to work on a Monday morning so I could spend the entire weekend there. I bought guides, read blogs, gathered tips and explored the city, and, for the first time, started imagining a life there. There was something about the old buildings, quaint streets, brasseries and the people that started to seduce me. I began to understand the fascination so many foreigners have with the city, where past and present collide on almost every street corner. I could see why so many dream of moving here and carving out their own slice of *la vie Parisienne*. The city began to speak to me. I could appreciate why James Thurber described it as 'a vast university of Art, Literature and Music . . . a seminar, a post-graduate course in everything'. Paris was educating me, widening my horizons and fine-tuning my aspirations. It was also opening my eyes to a new way of seeing and living. Walking home from dinner one evening, after six months of spending every other weekend there, I said that I wouldn't mind moving to Paris. And that was that. In January 2013, after a year of dating, I quit my job, packed up my London life and bought a one-way Eurostar ticket to settle in my new home and embark on the biggest adventure of my life.

It wasn't easy at first. No new life is, when you leave friends, family and all that you know behind. I didn't speak the language, nor did I have a defined career mapped out in my new city – but it was an opportunity. After nearly a year of living in my new home and adjusting a little more to my surroundings, I decided to start a blog. I had dabbled with one in London, but I hadn't really known what I wanted it to be, so quickly gave up. Moving to a new country – and to arguably the world's most beautiful city – gave me something to write about, and I named my blog after the first street I lived on: Rue Rodier. In the beginning, the blog was a creative outlet, purely an online journal. I used it to document my life in Paris, and as a space where I could publish my photographs – it was my own little corner of the internet. As I began to feel more comfortable in my new home, I started exploring more of my interests, namely style and interiors.

Thanks to my blog and my growing Instagram account, which was gaining a following from men and women who were interested in my life in Paris, I began meeting other like-minded expats and creatives who had either followed their hearts here (like me) or (unlike me) had always dreamed of living in this city. Paris played a huge role in the development of my new career, and it still does. It's thanks to living in Paris that I started contributing to sites and publications like Apartment Therapy and *Domino* magazine in the US about interiors; why I started getting some press in places like *Condé Nast Traveler*; and also why I began writing about Parisian style for Who What Wear in 2019. Today I am frequently asked for tips on style, interiors and beauty, along with my favourite spots in the city and what it's like to live in Paris – all things that have inspired me to write this book.

Moving to Paris was the catalyst I needed to make a change and set myself on the right path: a path that forced me to rethink and re-evaluate my life, and to finally follow my dreams. Back in London, for various reasons, I was scared to leave my comfort zone. I'd started working in publishing because, besides my love of books, it seemed (next to journalism) the best thing to do considering my skills and experience. I followed rules; I always listened to my parents (not that that's a bad thing, but our parents are human, too, and they don't *always* know what's best for us) and I stayed in my lane. I never really pushed or challenged myself. There were hints of it while I was living in East London, where I began to dabble more in my interests, but I never truly believed that I could make any significant changes, so I didn't. Moving to Paris was the motivation I needed to finally push my boundaries. Aptly, because this is a French phrase, it became my *raison d'être*. Coming here catapulted me into the unknown, and therefore it didn't matter if I tried new things or started again. It gave me the confidence I needed to choose a more rewarding path. I was indeed, as Guitry puts it, 'reborn' in Paris.

I've become – without meaning to or aiming to – a fully-fledged Francophile and practising Parisienne. My relationship with Paris has, so far, been the most important relationship of my life: I've learned to speak its language, to communicate with it, and to navigate its strange quirks and eccentricities. At times, I've happily compromised in order to be able to build a life and career here – perhaps because I had no prior expectations, no adolescent fantasies or lifelong dreams of what it would be like to live here. I came here as a blank canvas and have, thus far, painted myself with all the good, bad and ugly that Paris has to offer. And I say ugly, because despite what countless films and series might lead you to believe, Paris can be an unforgiving place to live (as can any city). It hasn't all been berets, baguettes and bouquets of peonies. Like any relationship, mine with Paris has had its ups and downs. There were times, in the beginning, when I didn't speak the language, and had few friends and little to no work, that I nearly threw in the towel. At the end of 2019, after another failed relationship, I even wondered if Paris was really still the place for me. But I'm glad I stayed. It's been a test of perseverance, as is any new life, challenge or adventure. And I'm all the richer for it. Over the years, Paris has become the place where I feel most at home. It is where, as Hepburn's character in *Sabrina* declares in a letter to her father, I 'have learned how to live . . . how to be in the world and of the world, and not just to stand aside and watch'. I believe there's much that the city and its inhabitants can teach all of us.

Sadly, the relationship I moved to Paris for didn't last, but after eight years living in the French capital and experiencing all the highs and lows the city has to offer, I have come to believe that Parisians do indeed do it better.

And by 'it', I do mean all the usual tropes associated with Parisians – like style, beauty and interiors – but also the things that make up the stuff of life, like love and relationships. Thanks to the Parisians, I have learned how to choose a good bottle of wine, what to wear and what to put on my face, but living in Paris has also taught me to be more curious, to take things less seriously, to make the most of life and to not sweat the small stuff. For me, practising Parisienne is practising *joie de vivre*. Because to me, to be Parisienne and embrace all that this city has to offer is to adopt a certain outlook on life – and I will show you how.

Many of Paris's most famous personalities and icons throughout history weren't born here. Some of them, such as Marie Antoinette or Jane Birkin, weren't even French, but found their place in life thanks to living in Paris. The same goes for many of my expat friends who now call Paris home: thanks to the city and all she has to offer, they have created lives for themselves that might not have been possible had they remained in the countries where they grew up. And even if, for some reason, we one day leave, I believe, as Hemingway famously wrote: 'Wherever you go for the rest of your life, it stays with you, for Paris is a moveable feast.' Paris has been the perfect place for me to explore and experiment with my passions and interests. It's no wonder so many famous artists and writers have at some point in their lives lived here – and why so many still dream of living here, despite how hard the reality of it can sometimes be.

Coming home

I've fallen in love with this city. I love the historical Haussmannian buildings, the beautiful five- and six-storey buildings lining the city's boulevards that were built in the second half of the nineteenth century and are one of the main reasons Paris is so easy on the eye. I love them even though they are constantly being renovated –

I once went without natural light in my apartment for two months while the building's façade was being repaired. I love the tiny apartments, which are rarely big enough to do a star jump in, and I'm not bothered anymore by the nineteenth-century electricity (which, on a visit to my last apartment in the 11ᵗʰ arrondissement, my dad said would be illegal in the UK). I have even come to love the grimy, often smelly, littered streets – the ones they don't show in films. I'm still bemused when I get beeped at, or even sworn at, by motorists when I have the audacity to cross the street when the green man is showing – but I love the fact that Parisians are not afraid to express and show emotions, which can bubble over in any situation. I've even come to develop an affection for the smelly metro stations that reek of what I like to call *'eau de Paris'* (okay, perhaps not, but you get my point – even its negatives somehow add to the city's charm). And, of course, I relish the colourful food markets, neighbourhood cafés, beautifully designed parks, and the smell of freshly baked baguettes that really does waft through the doors of the *boulangeries*. I adore the tiny, intimate restaurants that force you to keep your elbow movements to a minimum so you don't knock over your neighbour's glass of wine. (On that note, have you ever wondered why brasserie chairs face outwards towards the pavement? It's so that the customers can people-watch! Staring is a popular pastime in Paris, and one that you will get used to – and very good at – if you live here long enough.)

This book is, therefore, not just a book about Paris and how to be a little more Parisian: it is also my own personal story, about the challenges I've faced living in a foreign country, navigating its language and the bureaucracy (hint – there's a lot); it's about what I've learned from the city and its inhabitants, and how I believe living here has undoubtedly changed me for the better. This is a 'betterness' I'm not sure I could have achieved had I stayed in London. It's why the by-line to my blog is 'The road to better living'. Because Paris is where I believe my life took a turn for the better. There is something about its ambience and its people – their way of living, their *joie de vivre* – which is infectious, illuminating and life-affirming. I can totally relate to what Julia Child felt when she stated: 'I had come to the conclusion that I must really be French, only no one had ever informed me of this fact. I loved the people, the food, the lay of the land, the civilised atmosphere, and the generous pace of life.'

A celebration

'Be curious, in the sense of being sensitive to everything
– food, cinema, music. Try to expose yourself to things
that give you pleasure. Pleasure is essential'
Joseph Dirand

I know that there have been many books written about
Paris – its clichés, myths, how to be Parisian, what to
wear, how to wear it – but not many have been penned
by a British woman, particularly one who had never har-
boured a burning desire to live in this city. So I decided
to write one, and reveal everything that I've learned in
the eight years since I moved to the French capital. If
you've picked up this book, chances are you're either a
lover of Paris, or curious about what it's really like to
live here, clichés aside. So I'm going to explore the topics
and themes that I believe make up *la vie Parisienne* and
what you can learn from them. I will share all the things
that have enriched my life and that I believe can and
will enrich yours. I'm going to take you on my Parisian
journey via a few of my favourite subjects, namely style,
beauty, interiors, food, wine and love, with tips and
interviews from some of my favourite Parisians (some of
whom have always lived here, and others who, like me,
have adopted the city as their new home). My aim is to

show how you, too, can adopt a more Parisian attitude towards life.

I'm not saying that you should suddenly quit your job, pack your bags and move to Paris (although I certainly wouldn't stop you), but I do think that by adopting a few elements of *la vie Parisienne*, you can make some very positive changes to your daily life that will allow you to enjoy it to the best of your ability. As Joseph Dirand so beautifully puts it, pleasure is indeed essential. What, if anything, are we on this planet to do (with minimal damage), but to enjoy life and make the most of it? There aren't many people that I've encountered who are better at enjoying life than the Parisians.

Ultimately, this book is a celebration of the city that I call home, and also of the experience of living in a foreign place. If you ever have an excuse to move to another country, take it! Jump at the chance. I cannot tell you how enriching it is to immerse yourself in a new culture, make new friends and perhaps explore a new career opportunity. It will open your mind, expand your horizons and, most of all, it will teach you things about yourself that you may never have discovered had you always stayed in the same place. Ultimately, *Practising Parisienne* is a love letter to my home – Paris, the City of Lights – and its people. I hope you will enjoy coming on this journey with me.

The Parisian pace of life

The term *'flâneur'*, meaning 'stroller' or 'loafer' was invented in Paris by the nineteenth-century poet Charles Baudelaire, while Victor Hugo once said: 'To err is human. To loaf is Parisian.' The more generous pace of life is one of the things I love most about living in Paris. For example, when it comes to holidaying, nobody does it quite like the Parisians. I have never before lived in a city where almost the entire population migrates south for the month of August. Even restaurants, *boulangeries* and cafés shut up shop for as many as four weeks over the summer. With the Mediterranean on their doorstep and multiple holiday destinations, including Provence, Saint Tropez, and the Côte d'Azur just a train ride away, Parisians are perfectly placed to fully *profiter* (enjoy) their time off. This is not to say that they don't work hard the rest of the year – they do – it's just that they also take time off and make the most of it. And despite being eligible for nearly six to seven weeks of holiday and being absent for almost an entire month over the summer, France is one of the world's most economically successful countries.

I put it down to the fact that taking this time off allows the French to return to work fully rested, refreshed and ready to be productive for the rest of the year. It's something I believe the rest of the world can learn from.

A conversation with Vanessa Grall

Vanessa (@messynessychic) moved to Paris ten years ago, and launched her website, Messy Nessy Chic, not long after she arrived. This website, which she describes as a 'cabinet of chic curiosities', is where she writes about the weird and wonderful things she's found in Paris, along with its hidden history and anything ranging from crazy kitsch lighting to a beginners' guide to Italian ghost towns. She's also the author of a series of city guides called *Don't Be a Tourist*, which includes Paris and New York editions.

You describe yourself as a storyteller, collector and forgotten history lover. How did moving to Paris inspire what you do today?

> I think moving to any new city opens your eyes (I highly recommend it if you're ever in a rut). The urban unknown automatically makes you more curious, especially with a city like Paris, which has so many layers. I like to think of Paris as my muse. With so much history all around you – Paris being its own open-air museum – you can't ignore the city's past, so I also found myself suddenly becoming quite nostalgic for eras that I felt I had 'missed'. I was aware, too, that my new home had this very iconic status, but I found myself more interested in finding out what it wasn't so famous for. This combination of curiosity for the unknown, and the opportunity to revive stories lost in time and translation took me down the rabbit hole that I'm lucky enough to call my career so far.

What do you love most about living in Paris?

Oh, lots of things. Aside from its beauty, I love the pace of life.
There is a lack of pressure, yet an emphasis on being creative.
If I'm honest, I'm not very ambitious in the traditional sense. I
like to dream, do what I love and hope for the best, and I think
Paris has worked out quite well for me in that respect.

Why do you think Paris is so alluring?

Paris has been the centre of all things desirable and glamorous
for centuries. Fashion, of course, is one France's greatest
exports, and to think about what made Paris the centre of
fashion for the past 300 years, you've got to think about the
entire culture of it – the depth and sophistication – not just
the iconic designers and their muses. It involved a whole cast
of sophisticated fashion performers and spectators: artists,
artisans, writers, tastemakers, *flâneurs*, filmmakers, actors and
influencers, all of whom played a role in making Paris this
legendary centre of style.

**What has living in Paris taught you about life? And how do you
think the Parisian lifestyle can inspire others?**

One of the first things I noticed is that there's less of a
tendency to 'show off' here by wearing designer labels, being
seen in the hottest restaurants or driving flashy cars. You
might even say that Parisians have a sense of shyness or
even embarrassment when it comes to having expensive and
materialistic things. I'll admit I'm pretty happy to have been
cured of my desire for designer handbags. But, to be fair, Paris
has a lot to learn from New York and London, too, and you
can see it sort of borrowing certain aspects of those cities – a
little bit of Brooklyn here, a little bit of Brick Lane there. As I

said, I prefer the pace of life here, which is something that I
think London and New York lack – a kind of herd acceptance
that things don't need to be working 24/7 – and that's okay,
because here the simple pleasures of life are held in high
regard.

Do you have any tips on how to get the most out of Paris?
Parisians are curious. Be imaginative. Don't just go to the
places and sites that are expected of you. Instead, seek out
things to do that align with your own passions and your
interests. And if you're still finding out what those things
are, why not pick a character (real or fictional) who has your
dream job – make it something unique – and research Paris
pretending that you were that person. What would they do?
Where would they go? You'd be surprised how many peculiar
places you'll discover.

What are your favourite places in Paris?
I love secret restaurants, but the real Mom & Pop finds, not
so much the faux speakeasy ones where they make you walk
through a fridge door! La Maison De La Culture Arménienne
in the 9th arrondissement, for example, has absolutely zero
indication of a restaurant behind the street entrance at 17 rue
Bleue. Follow the comforting smell of simmering onions and
spices up to the first floor, where you'll find the warmest
welcome in Paris. Just like at home, there's no menu, but
your newly adopted 'Mama Armenia' will suggest the dishes
of the day, which always include their special recipe for juicy
dumplings. The no-frills setting is recompensed by stories of a
culturally diverse Paris on the walls.

As for my favourite shop, not so long ago, there was a

kind old man named Roger who ran a tiny antiques shop stuck to the side of a church in the heart of Paris's most luxurious shopping district. He had a curious collection of trinkets for sale – made even more curious by the fact that he also sold fresh eggs, brought in daily from his farm outside the city. When I heard Roger had retired, I was sure his little shop would be overtaken by a soulless luxury boutique. But its new occupant, Brigitte Tanaka, is just as whimsical as the last. Having kept Roger's shop exactly as they found it, the talented French and Japanese duo behind Brigitte Tanaka have filled this unique store with delightfully curated vintage pieces and upcycled antiques, unique accessories and charming homewares. It's quite the little jewel box.

My favourite place to surprise Parisians (or visitors) is the Petit Palais in the 8th arrondissement. Most people have no idea about the urban oasis hidden inside the Petit Palais museum, which is just off the Champs Elysées. A good part of my book *Don't be a Tourist in Paris* was written right here, in a café that feels worlds away from the city. The covered marble terrace overlooking the exotic garden is writer's magic. Not so '*petit*', the museum itself is also a favourite of mine, a great alternative to the Orsay or the Louvre. They have all the greats – Monet, Renoir, Cezanne – and you practically have the place to yourself most days. (And it's free!)

A conversation with Samar Seraqui de Buttafoco

Samar (@ulap) was born in the Ivory Coast and left at the age of 15 for an internship in Lebanon, then later moved to Paris. While she's not French, she says she feels 'viscerally French in thought'. She's a former journalist (she worked on the Arab-speaking desk of *France 24*) and was one of France's first influencers. She began blogging about fashion in 2009 through her blog Une Libanaise à Paris. In 2017, she launched her T-shirt brand, Das Mot, and in the last few years she's been very involved with charity work. Most recently, she raised 89,000€ to help the people of Beirut in the aftermath of the explosion in August 2020. To me, she embodies the Parisienne who wasn't born in Paris, but who has made the most of life in the City of Lights.

What does being a Parisienne mean to you?

Paris is a choice; we don't come here by chance, and everyone has his or her own story to tell. Living in Paris also means living in the capital of human rights. This is a free city where everyone can live their life in the way they want to. The Parisian fascinates, but Paris is not a Godard film.

What have you experienced during your life in Paris that you might not have learned or done if you had stayed in Lebanon, for example?

Coeducation. Also, I would not have met people who are different from me and who come from different countries. However, I don't think the city's inhabitants have the same sense of community you find in cities like London, New York or Milan; I have very few Lebanese friends here, for example.

What do you think Parisian life can teach foreigners?

Paris teaches us taste. At first glance, it is a very difficult city to live in, and the reception can be cold, unlike in other capitals or large cities. But, with a little patience and time, connections are made – and I think these connections are more genuine and less about flattery.

Why do you think Parisian life is so interesting for foreigners?

The baguette, social security, good wine – and, of course, *la liberté*: freedom.

What about you? Why Paris?

I literally dream in French, so Paris was an obvious choice for me. Paris is my base; from here I have discovered France and I can travel the world. My blog also helped me with this.

What are your favourite places in Paris?

I like to walk along the quays of la Seine and cross the bridges between the left and right banks. I also love the Giacometti Foundation and the Musée d'Orsay. I enjoy sitting down in my little café with silver bushes on Rue du Bac. I also like to take refuge in La Madeleine church when it's too hot – and I love having lunch at Huguette.

Style & fashion

Fashion lives in Paris

'Paris dictates fashion to the whole world'
Maria Callas

Paris can be characterised by many things: its tree-lined boulevards, framed by the city's iconic Haussmannian buildings, with their beige facades and zinc roofs; the Tour Eiffel, which stands watch over its inhabitants; its famous cafés, where once sat Hemingway, Proust and Picasso; its *boulangeries*, whose breads are the backbone of the country's cuisine; or perhaps by the river Seine, that runs through the city like an artery, coming to life during the summer as Parisians take to its banks for picnics and al fresco *apéros*. For me, though, Paris is most simply and profoundly illustrated through its style: by the fashion in the streets and on the terraces; by the clothes worn by its people. It's through their style and accessory choices that I believe Paris's true identity is brought to life – an identity that seeps into all of the aforementioned aspects in *la vie Parisienne*. It is no coincidence that one of the most famous opera singers of the last century, Maria Callas, made the sweeping statement above, and it's a claim that can still be made today.

Fashion lives everywhere in the French capital – it's part of the furniture, so to speak, and makes up a living,

breathing part of Parisian life. As Coco Chanel so elo-
quently said: 'Fashion is not something that exists in
dresses only. Fashion is in the sky, in the street. Fashion
has to do with ideas, the way we live, what is happening.'
And in my opinion, there is no city in the world where
this rings more true than in Paris. That's why this explor-
ation of its fashion and style forms the first section of
my book, as my journey towards becoming one of Paris's
residents wouldn't be complete without it; I've learned so
much from the inhabitants of this city through their style
and how they outwardly present themselves.

When researching for this book, it came as no surprise
to me to learn that Paris has had a serious long-term relationship with fashion for nearly 400 years. Its *histoire*,
as the French say (meaning, in this case, 'relationship'),
dates back to King Louis XIV, France's longest-reigning
monarch, who took up his throne in 1643 and made it
one of his missions to make Paris the fashion capital of
the world. He did so with such success that his finance
minister, Jean-Baptiste Colbert, famously declared, 'fashion is to France what the gold mines of Peru are to Spain'.
Louis XIV paved the way for the fashion landscape of
Paris today, – and for its many *maisons* – Chanel, Dior,
Hermès, Celine and Balenciaga, to name a few. Many of
fashion's most iconic moments were made in Paris, and
I could spend hours listing them here, but I'll leave that
for another time – or another book. Needless to say, when
you think of great style, you probably think of Paris and
the Parisians.

Parisians – or at least, Paris-based designers – also have the ability to force a minor trend into the mainstream. Consider the bicycle short – a trend that has been a little under the radar for the last few years, mainly worn by influencers and editors at the forefront of the fashion industry, until Anthony Vaccarello, Creative Director of YSL, included a bicycle short in his spring/summer '21 collection. It was the main item that Charlotte Gainsbourg, Lily Collins, Kais Gerber and Blackpink's Rosé all chose to wear from the new collection. Part of the reason for this may be that Parisian style is notably more restrained than the fashions of other cities of note, so once something becomes a trend in Paris, it is deemed acceptable for the rest of world to follow suit.

The myth of Parisian style

'Fashions fade, style is eternal'
Yves Saint Laurent

There is a tendency to pigeonhole and stereotype Parisian style – I know I've been doing it for years. But I don't think that's really a bad thing. For decades, we've been inundated with the same ideas. There's the image of the red-lipped Parisian woman in a white shirt and jeans, who wears a beret in winter, a trench in spring and espadrilles in summer – a fire ignited by past style icons such as Brigitte Bardot and Jane Birkin, and one that is fuelled today by France's Insta-stars, many of whom have become famous perhaps because they resemble these women. Then there's the classic *'Le Smoking'*, a tuxedo-style masculine black suit created by Yves Saint Laurent in the sixties and immortalised in black and white by the famed photographer Helmut Newton. *'Le Smoking'* was the designer's contemporary answer to Chanel's 'Little Black Dress', but its bold bending of genders shook femininity to the core, and it became one of the first examples of 'power dressing'. In doing so, it also catapulted Parisian style towards iconic status. The suit was donned by Catherine Deneuve and Loulou de la Falaise, who both modelled for Laurent at the height of their fame and was borrowed by the likes of Bianca Jagger. It has come to be seen as Parisian style personified, celebrated by the likes of Lou Dillon and Caroline de Maigret (Karl Lagerfeld's former muse), as well as more recent influencers, such as Leia Sfez. Incidentally, Anthony Vaccarello revived the iconic image when he created an ode to '*Le Smoking*' for the YSL Spring/Summer '20 campaign, which proves just how timeless it is, and just how important these archetypes are to Parisian style.

These are two very different examples of Parisian style clichés, one a little more cutesy and saccharine, the other brooding, masculine and mysterious. But they play a key role in representing our concept of Parisian fashion, and we can be forgiven for wanting to wear them – they are just as relevant today as they were then. Then, of course, there's the blue-and-white striped Breton top, an item originally worn by fishermen that was adopted by the French navy in 1858, and then made famous by none other than Chanel herself. It has since gained the title of 'wardrobe classic': there aren't many Parisiennes without a version in their closet, and it's been replicated by a multitude of brands. So you see, it's easy to stereotype Parisian style, but that's because iconic French fashion consists of a few key items that have stood the test of time. At its heart, French style is simple, and these simple classics stand out because they are easy to wear. And why not? After all, if it ain't broke . . . In my interview with Monica de La Villardière later in this section, she admits to owning many of the items that her grandmother wore during her time in Paris in the forties, because they are still relevant and stylish today. It's one of the reasons that classic Parisian style hasn't really changed all that much since the sixties, when Jane Birkin was its icon.

Of course, there are some stereotypes that don't quite live up to reality, like the idea of Parisian women wearing high heels. Unless you are, say, a French fashion editor or influencer, and being taken from A to B in a chauffeur-driven car, the image of a French woman pounding the Parisian pavements in her stilettos is, I've learned, pure fiction. Paris is a walking city and, with its uneven pavements and cobbled streets, it's not one made for heels. The truth is that French girls' footwear choices are decidedly more practical. Thanks to what I've learned from the Parisiennes, I can't remember the last time I tottered precariously down the street, attempting to walk tall in skyscraper stilettos on an evening out. I often have to tell my English friends (who are more accustomed to wearing high heels for a night on the town) to pack comfortable shoes and low heels for the evenings when they come to visit me.

As I said earlier, I've been guilty myself of keeping some of these clichés alive. I've written about Parisian style and how to replicate it for *Who What Wear*. I, too, carry basket bags (they are practical for market shopping) and wear espadrilles in summer (they're comfortable, look good and are great on grass – so good for garden weddings). I have been known to wear berets in winter (they are a chic way to keep your head warm). I often wrap myself up in a trench coat when the seasons turn from winter to spring. I think suits look great on women, and an oversized, slightly masculine black blazer is one of the most hard-working items in my wardrobe. I cannot discount these clichés, because they remain popular for a reason: they are classic, easy to wear, and effortlessly chic.

Parisian style de-coded

> *'The signature item is an attitude.*
> *It is the gun in your holster that makes you*
> *feel well dressed and invincible'*
> **Caroline de Maigret,** *How to be Parisian*

Parisian style is often said to embody the famous phrase, *je ne sais quoi*. One can put it down to an attitude, one that is a little more confident, nonchalant and defiant. As Garance Doré writes in her book *Love Style Life*, 'the French woman says no'. The French have never been afraid to say what they think (I often see this with my friends) or fight for what they believe in – I have never lived in a city where they protest more than Paris. It's an attitude that dates back to the French Revolution. And they have a habit of breaking the rules. During the coronavirus outbreak, the French prime minister noted that Parisians do not follow rules. This was one of the main reasons we went into strict lockdowns where we needed to sign an *attestation* – a permission slip stating our reason for leaving the house, which allowed us to be outside for only one hour, and within a 1km radius of home.

Despite the Parisian fondness for loudly expressing their opinions, their dress sense is, on the whole, a little quieter – perhaps because they do not need to let their outward appearance do the talking. This is a sentiment that has been keenly confirmed to me on various occasions when discussing fashion with Parisian friends. Their sense of style lies in simplicity and a wardrobe of essentials. Fashion weeks aside, I have never walked down a street in Paris and seen the array of colours and outlandish outfits that I do in London. And there are rarely grunge, goth or punk looks – for Parisiennes, their appearances are not outward displays of their internal angst. The same goes for beauty (more on this later): I don't have a single Parisian friend who has dyed her hair pink, bright red or – *mon dieu!* – blue. One could say it's rather restrained and boring, but I like to think of it as refined. Parisiennes prefer to rely on their characters and personalities, rather than trying to express themselves through crazy clothing and extreme beauty choices.

That's not to say they don't have fun with fashion; it's just that they generally prefer to have their opinions heard and let their personalities speak for themselves. Of course I have Parisian friends who rebel against the classic notion of Parisian style, such as Ellie of @slipintostyle on Instagram, who I speak to on page 78 (but, after all, she *is* Parisian – it is her prerogative to break the rules).

This love of simplicity could also be a result of rejecting excess – a hangover from the French Revolution. As Monica de La Villardière, who I interview on page 82, explains, 'to be selective is to be chic'. There is so much choice and excess in Paris, so part of being chic is to curate a lifestyle from carefully selected items. In my opinion, there is no other collective of people better at paring back and carefully curating their lives than the Parisiennes: another reason why I am writing this book.

I've tried to break it down many times: our fascination with the Parisian woman and the way she dresses. It appears to be simple, much like her style – the appeal lies in the 'effortlessness' of it all, the laid-back way in which she dresses. It is far less try-hard than the majority of the world's fashions. Stereotypes aside, I do think there is a sort of 'uniform' that can be deciphered, and we'll look at this in more detail soon. But what's more important is the woman wearing the clothes: her apparent confidence and indifference to the opinions of others. Although she does care, she wants you to think that she doesn't. She dresses for herself and doesn't fervently follow trends. This makes her style easier to replicate, because she isn't rigidly trying to keep up to date with the latest looks coming off the catwalks, but at the same time it is unique, because she's dressing for herself and for her mood that day (as I discuss later on with both Deborah Sebag Reyner, page 59, and Anne-Laure Mais, page 74). Ultimately, Parisiennes wear what flatters their shape and what makes them feel comfortable and confident. They will only wear trends that complement what they already have in their wardrobe.

So if you have trouble getting dressed in the morning, and often find yourself staring blankly into the back of your wardrobe, wasting precious time while you contemplate what on earth to wear that day, then taking a Parisian approach can save you time – and money – in the long run.

Earlier, I mentioned the contrast between Paris and London fashions, noting that us Brits are generally more experimental in colour and dress sense. This is something I discussed with Monica during our interview (see page 82), and a question she and her *Fashion No Filter* podcast partner, Camille Charrière, the London-based Parisian, style icon, influencer and writer, addressed in their show for Paris Première. It's not just down to the influence of the punk era in London. They put it down to the fact that in the UK, we have school uniform, whereas French children can wear whatever they like to class. From this, they came to the conclusion that because the Parisiennes had choice as children, they created their own uniform in rebellion against *not* wearing one when they were younger. This could indeed be a reason. Looking back at my school-uniform days, I certainly remember that when, in year ten, aged fifteen, we were allowed to wear coloured shirts instead of the regulation starched white, I began expressing myself more earnestly through the things I wore – because I was bored with the school uniform. I started introducing jumpers and accessories to help differentiate myself from my fellow students. I donned an Ellesse zipper jacket (instead of one by Kappa, which was the favourite brand at the time), for example, to help express some kind of individuality – and thus began my years of fashion experimentation, until I moved to Paris. And I imagine, if we follow Monica and Camille's theory, that Parisiennes did the opposite – paring back their style as they reached adulthood, as they'd perhaps already done more experimenting in their youth.

My style story

> 'Dress shabbily, and they remember the dress;
> dress impeccably, and they remember the woman'
> **Coco Chanel**

To talk about how living in Paris has transformed my
personal style, I feel I need to start at the beginning and
set the scene to give you a better idea of where I was
coming from. I had never looked towards our French
cousins for fashion advice. In fact, growing up, I never
really looked anywhere for fashion advice. I never flicked
through fashion magazines as a teenager, as I imagine
others working within the fashion industry today did. I
didn't buy *Vogue* – I'm not sure I even knew it existed
until I watched *Sex and the City* in my late teens. As an
only child, with no older siblings to pave the way, and an
overly protective mother who wouldn't let me get the bus
to school until I was fourteen, I grew up pretty sheltered
from the outside world. So it was my mum, family friends
and my peers at school who inspired my clothing choices.

I never really thought about the concept of styles when
I was a teenager, apart from considering how I could be
cooler and fit in at the all-girls school I attended (which
I never managed to do very well). I did, however, like
beautiful things and art. As a kid, I was dragged around

galleries by my dad, a gift I will always be grateful for now. But somehow, as so many teenagers do, either through osmosis or peer pressure (probably the latter), I did manage to keep up with current trends (if you can call nineties style a 'trend' – still a contentious topic today). Circa 1996, at age fourteen, I remember being a Kula Shaker-inspired hippy (if you too were going through puberty in the early nineties, you might remember the band). I went through a stage of wearing flares so big, they covered my feet; in fact, that was the whole point. If they didn't envelop my entire foot, they weren't cool. I would pair these flares with some sort of emblazoned T-shirt, a knitted multi-coloured cross-body bag and beads. Oh, and let's not forget the red leather biker jacket. And then there were the Posh-Spice-wannabe outfits, when I would wear a leopard print 'going out' top (they've made a recent comeback), paired with an elasticated mini skirt, platform heels and no coat (even in the dead of winter). This was donned for the weekly pilgrimage to the local nightclub, Churchills, aka 'Chills', on a Friday night when I was seventeen.

I began to follow fashion more fervently at around the age of twenty-six, when I moved in with two friends in a block of flats just off Mare Street in Hackney, East London. It was there that I really let lose in my experimentation of style (as many do when they move to the area) – I was probably trying to 'find myself' through clothes, alongside some other extracurricular activities that I won't discuss here. Living there, I was more exposed to fashion, not just because the area was (and still is) a creative hub for artists, musicians and others in the fashion crowd, but also because both friends and flatmates worked as buyers – one for ASOS and the other for Net-a-Porter – and therefore they were usually so impeccably well-dressed that I was forced to step up my game for fear of looking shabby next to them, or being labelled the 'non-fashion' friend. Yet I didn't develop a better sense of style – weirder and more colourful, yes, but not *better*. One example that sticks out in my memory, much to my dismay, is a long-sleeved multi-coloured psychedelic print dress from H & M, which was undeniably the dress version of the Zap ice lollies I used to love as a kid. I thought it was *très cool*. My buyer friend and her colleague, on the other hand, did not. I can distinctly remember them eyeing me up on the Tube to work one morning, and I could tell they felt a little embarrassed by my choice of outfit, and perhaps somewhat blinded by my colourful presence. It looked like someone had thrown up a bag of Skittles all over me.

Given my lack of personal style and slapdash choices in clothing, when I moved to Paris I felt like a duck out of water, but with time and a lot of trial and error, I've finally refined my sense of style. While I developed a keen interest in fashion while living in London, it has undoubtedly been while living in Paris that I have learned how to *dress*.

Curating a Parisian wardrobe

'I will always go to things that make me feel comfortable'
Isabel Marant

When I moved to Paris, I plunged my wardrobe into a morbid monochrome palette of mainly black, despite my history of making more kaleidoscopic clothing choices. I was baffled by what to wear and intimidated by suddenly finding myself in the fashion capital of the world. It was as if my wardrobe choices were the physical manifestations of the insecurities I was feeling. They mirrored how out of place I felt in my new city, not to mention my lack of French, and so these clothes were an attempt to blend in.

The stonewashed high-waisted nineties vintage jeans, paired with a bat-winged, sequined knit from Rokit and white Reebok high-tops that I'd worn in my old neighbourhood in Dalston weren't going to cut it in the city where elegance and good taste reign supreme. We Brits are not afraid of a little bad taste, happy to indulge in clashing colours and crazy prints. It's not a bad thing: it's one of our strengths, and many Parisiennes I've talked to love the freedom of style and self-expression they see in London. But in Paris, it's a very different story. I didn't want to stick out like a sore thumb. Plus, I was going into my thirtieth year, and thought it high time I learned how to dress in a way a little more suited to my age, figure and personality. I wanted to be revered for my style, not stared at.

After some experimentation (and a few further fashion faux pas), I've finally learned how to dress a little more effortlessly. I no longer try to disappear *or* stand out, nor do I try to actively follow trends. I don't overdress like I did in my London days – here, overdressing is a big *NON*. Instead, I have adopted a more timeless, grown-up style. I've swapped high-tops for Supergas, and finally found the right jeans to flatter my figure. As I pared back my wardrobe, opting for a more sober palette of black, white, grey and navy, I learned how to affectively navigate the Parisian art of dressing. And as I slowly reintroduced a little more colour, print and texture into my closet, taking in style inspiration from the streets and Parisian friends, I started noticing that certain items have come to make up the pillars of my Parisian closet. A pattern started to emerge – a code, if you will – and it's one that forms the foundation of every Parisian wardrobe. Elodie Fagan, who used to work at Pinterest France and worked on the launch of the site in the French market, says: 'We realised that when it came to style, French people were operating within a very codified, nominative culture – basically, you have to express strong individual style within a very limited choice of brands and colours. So women were telling us, "I can dress in *beige, blanc, noir*, and then I can dress within these five brands that are acceptable.

45

But within these five colours and five brands, I have to express strong individual style."' While all Parisian wardrobes are built around the same key items, such as the cardigan, the white shirt and the high-waisted jean, each Parisienne still expresses her own unique style in the way she wears them. These are items that Parisian brands such as Sézane, Isabel Marant, ba&sh, Balzac and Rouje have built their successful businesses around.

And so I've learned how to curate a capsule wardrobe, and in the pages that follow I will help you build your own collection of timeless yet stylish essentials and investment pieces that my fellow Parisiennes would be proud of. I will talk to fashion friends I admire, such as my fellow expat Monica de La Villardière, a *British Vogue* contributor, Elle.fr correspondent and podcast host; Anne-Laure Mais, founder and creative director of the brand Musier; stylist Deborah Reyner Sebag; founder of Balzac Paris, Chrysoline de Gastines; and influencer Ellie Delphine. We will explore the lessons I've learned, including the most important: how to dress for your own body, and how to wear clothing that flatters and fits you rather than just conforming to a seasonal trend. Of course you can still follow trends, just don't let them completely dictate your buying choices. A strong wardrobe inspired by Parisian style is crafted from pieces that have longevity and will last season after season, long after the trends have changed. Because of this, I also believe a Parisienne's wardrobe to be more sustainable – but more on that later.

Parisian style is simple

'Simplicity is the keynote of all true elegance'
Coco Chanel

Berets and Breton tops aside, I believe Parisian style boils down to a few key things: simplicity, figure-enhancing pieces and, most importantly, wearing items that are confidence-building and make you feel like yourself, not like you're trying to look like someone else. That's why Parisian style is so famous: it makes you look great and appear more confident. Take jeans, for example. A staple of the Parisian wardrobe, they can, if worn correctly for one's body type, do wonders for the figure (especially the *derrière*) – and they go with everything. Another good example is the white shirt, a timeless wardrobe staple that has been reinvented time and time again, most recently by Jacquemus. I challenge you to find a more iconic pairing than a white shirt, sleeves rolled up, loosely tucked into a pair of high-waisted, straight-legged jeans. It's iconic because it's simple, flattering and easy to replicate – and we do! Everyone has, at some point, sported this timeless ensemble, from *Vogue* editor-in-chief Emmanuelle Alt to Clémence Poésy and Leia Sfez. This simple, elegant approach is the ethos that iconic Parisian brands like A. P. C. were built on – the brand was initially created as 'a reaction to the over-designed and over-hyped seasonal fashion trends'. Even Isabel Marant – who, with her eponymous label, has designed clothes donned by the French 'cool girls' for the past two decades and whose creations are, on the whole, busier in terms of colour and pattern – creates collections that still incorporate the classics: jeans, trench, white shirt (albeit with a boho twist) and blazer.

Simple is more sustainable.
A note on sustainability

'When a woman says, "I have nothing to wear!",
what she really means is, "There's nothing here for
who I'm supposed to be today"'
Caitlin Moran

I first came across this quote when reading Lauren Bravo's book, *How to Break Up with Fast Fashion*, and I wanted to share it here because it sums up exactly what I want to say about sustainability with regards to Parisian fashion. This quote, from the British journalist and author Caitlin Moran, illustrates how I used to feel about my wardrobe, pre-Paris. I would stand there looking at my clothes, trying to choose the clothes that would reflect who I wanted to be that day. I felt the need to constantly change who I was, and the easiest way to do that was with the clothes I was wearing. But it was ultimately a disguise, and I never felt truly myself.

The problem with fashion is it tries to force us to constantly reinvent ourselves, with magazines telling us what we should wear next spring or next winter, according to the new collections released the season before. But what if we didn't have to? What if you didn't feel pressured to wear the latest look or express yourself entirely through the clothes that you wear? Hello, Parisian style.

As I explained earlier, a Parisian would rather speak up themselves than let their clothes do all the talking. I'm not against fashion trends, but by taking a page out of a Parisienne's book, you could also help to save the environment. If we, like the Parisiennes, chose to invest in timeless classics, there would be a lot less clothing ending up in landfill sites. One of my favourite things about Parisiennes is that they often loudly reject fast fashion in favour of more sustainable clothing that will have longevity. For example, many Parisian influencers, such as Sabina Socol, snub Black Friday and instead highlight just how wasteful this shopping event is in their Instagram posts. Parisiennes also have a penchant for vintage clothing, perhaps one of the reasons why the website Vestiaire Collective, which sells higher-end second-hand and vintage clothing and accessories, was born in Paris and has been so successful. It's not unusual for Parisiennes to inherit items from family members either, as investment-buying was something their mothers and grandmothers did before the rise of fast fashion. I often host *vide dressings* or 'closet clear-outs' to empty my wardrobe of anything I haven't worn for a while. I've held a few of these with friends to great success – as the saying goes, 'one (wo)man's trash is another (wo)man's treasure'. I'm a big believer in recycling, and the more clothes I can resell or find new homes for, the better! I'm not saying that Parisiennes never buy fast fashion – I have been known to go on a Zara binge every now and again – nor do they avoid following trends entirely, but I have learned the merit of saving up for a well-cut blazer that I can wear year after year and won't go out of fashion, thanks to its timeless understated style.

✤ TOP TIP ✤

Bookmark Vestiaire Collective, and download the Depop and Vinted apps. And if you want to be even more sustainable you can reduce your buying and rent instead from places like Rotaro, By Rotation, My Wardrobe HQ and Cocoon Club.

Chrysoline de Gastines' capsule wardrobe items

Chrysoline (@chrysoline_de_gastines) founded Balzac Paris in 2014 with her family. From the very beginning, she wanted to create a brand that does fashion differently. Sustainability and a commitment to the environment were huge drivers for her, as fashion is the second-biggest polluter in the world. She wanted to launch a brand that designs a limited series of timeless and classic collections to help women build a more responsible wardrobe, so they work by a simple philosophy: 'T.P.R: *Toujours Plus Responsible*' (always the most responsible). It's part of their brand DNA and at the centre of everything they do, whether that's the products, logistics, marketing or client services. This approach also filters into their relationships with the brand's collaborators. So I wanted to ask Chrysoline for her top three items to create a capsule wardrobe that lasts.

Jeans

I'll start with the jean – once the French find a jean that suits them, they will buy two to three of the same, as it's important to find a good silhouette and a cut that flatters the figure, as well as an item that they can wear for a long time. For example, we have a style at Balzac called Mattis, which is 100 per cent cotton, with no elastane – so the first time you wear them, they are a bit stiff, but it gives your behind a good shape. They're also not too skinny, which gives them a bit of a retro shape that can be worn all year round, for example with boots in winter and plimsolls or ballerinas in summer.

Shirt

The next item that I love is the shirt, because it's so versatile: you can put it on in the morning for work and then leave it on for the evening and just add a pretty bra or body underneath. The beauty of the shirt is in the neckline; a woman can choose to show as much décolletage or cleavage as she wants, by undoing some of the buttons. I love shirts and have many different styles in my wardrobe, both masculine and feminine, including striped, white, chambray and silk. I like to create a classic look with jeans and a belt – because a belt helps to create a nice silhouette. Or I'll pair one with a roll neck underneath. During the summer, a shirt is essential, because you can wear it to go out in and you can wear it over a swimming costume or bikini. It's a key French wardrobe piece as it gives off an air of nonchalance, and you can wear it for every occasion – to work, to go out and to the beach!

Sneakers

And finally, I'm a sneaker person. I like to wear jeans with a jumper and a pair of sneakers. I really like leopard-print accessories, for example, and think they work brilliantly with a white shirt and light blue jeans. For me, this is the silhouette – jeans, shirt and sneakers, that you can wear season after season and for every occasion.

Style lessons I've picked up from the Parisiennes

'Before you leave the house, look in the mirror and take one thing off. It is always better to be underdressed'
Coco Chanel

After eight years of rubbing shoulders with some of Paris's best dressed women, I have come to learn a few key lessons about style, including how to dress a little more elegantly and, ultimately, for myself, which makes me feel confident.

Less is always more – Parisiennes generally don't over-dress, which is one of the main reasons why jeans are such a staple clothing item, for both day and evening dressing. They can easily be dressed up with a cute top and blazer, or dressed down with sneakers, according to the occasion. To overdress is deemed a fashion faux pas and, just as their beauty regime adheres to the 'less is more' adage, Parisiennes tend to go easy on accessories, often opting to wear one carefully chosen accessory to elevate the entire look. I try to follow the advice from Coco Chanel I quoted at the beginning of this chapter, and remove one item.

Invest in items that last – This may seem like a no-brainer, but it's something that is all too often forgotten thanks to the overwhelming number of fast-fashion items on offer. If you want to build a wardrobe that lasts, you need to reach a little deeper into your wallet. When it comes to fashion, there is nothing more rewarding than saving up for something that you will actually keep and cherish for years to come. Investing in a better piece will also save you money later on.

Don't wear skyscraper heels – By all means, own a pair. Perhaps you might need them for a wedding one day, or an important event, if heels make you feel more confident or powerful, which they can certainly do (there's always a time and a place to be a little more *Working Girl* in my book). But this is not your go-to shoe. Low, block heels are your friends, as are loafers in winter and espadrilles in summer. Comfort is key when it comes to Parisian footwear.

Go easy on prints – Approach pattern with caution: go easy on prints and mainly wear them in summer. Prints date fast, and will rarely stand the test of time (except for leopard print, which is a fail-safe in a Parisienne's fashion book, and is generally regarded as a neutral). If you regularly buy from the high street, steer clear of bold prints – it's likely you'll see someone else walking towards you wearing exactly the same item. I know, because it happened to me multiple times when I was younger. Gingham and checks are also classics, as is tweed in winter à la Chanel. And on that note, there's nothing more timeless than a Chanel jacket: if you can afford to invest in one, you will have it for the rest of your life.

Shop vintage – While there is an undeniable Parisian dress code, Parisiennes like nothing better than finding a unique piece – and there's no better way to do that than shopping vintage. Plus, of course, it's better for the planet. There are dozens of shops dedicated to vintage clothing dotted around Paris, such as Kilo Shop and Hippy Market, but the Parisians are also good at treasure-hunting, so they will find pieces at local pop-up *brocantes* (flea markets) and online on sites such as eBay, Etsy, Vestiaire Collective, Vinted and Le Bon Coin (France's answer to Gumtree).

Borrow from the boys – Parisiennes have mastered the art of masculine dressing. After all, Paris was the birth-place of '*Le Smoking*', the suit I mentioned earlier. In my opinion, there's nothing sexier than wearing something a little oversized and slightly masculine that leaves more to the imagination. Wear an oversized shirt or jacket, but keep your underwear dainty and a little lacy. As the editor of *Vogue Paris* stated in Garance Doré's book *Love Style Life*, 'For me, femininity is in no way tied to wearing a dress or a skirt. I think you can be incredibly feminine in pants.'

Keep your accessories minimal and dainty – While big jewellery has its place – mainly at fashion week and retro parties – small, dainty and more discreet jewellery will go with everything, and it also looks more elegant. Invest in a few key items, or better yet have them gifted for birthdays or special occasions. Save up for a nice necklace or bracelet, preferably in sterling silver or solid gold – anything that won't make your skin go green. It's good to have options, but if you want to create a more minimal wardrobe with less fuss, the same should go for your accessories.

Your clothes should make you feel like *you* – Clothes should ultimately make you feel confident, sexy and yourself! Wearing something should not make you feel like you're trying to be someone else. Find items that flatter and accentuate your assets. As Isabel Marant once said: 'Most of all, feel self-confident. When you see people who are self-confident, they radiate something good."

There are no rules – I know I've essentially just shared a list of what could be seen as rules, but the truth is that if you do want to adopt a more Parisian approach to style, while you might adhere to a few principles, ultimately you should simply dress for yourself, your body type and your mood. Although in these pages I'm promoting a more refined sense of style, fashion is also meant to be fun, so enjoy it and choose what makes you feel good.

A style chat with Deborah Reyner Sebag

Deborah (@thedailydeb) is a fashion consultant, influencer and stylist contributing to the likes of *L'Officiel* and French *ELLE*. She also co-founded a ceramics brand called Vessel in 2020. I met her a few years ago during a lunch with GAP, and I remember ogling her Gucci loafers. She has since become a friend. I wanted to talk to her as she represents what I believe to be Parisian style, but she also follows the trends. She manages to stylishly combine staple, iconic Parisian pieces with the latest trends – without looking like a fashion victim.

How would you describe your style?
   Parisian and casual, but with a twist.
How would you describe Parisian style?
   A mix of wardrobe essentials worn with a 'mastered'
   nonchalance.
What are your Parisian wardrobe essentials ?
   A Breton striped top, a pair of vintage Levi's 501 straight jeans,
   a pair of loafers or moccasins, a white T-shirt, a men's shirt,
   an oversized blazer and a trench.
What or who inspires the way you dress?
   My daily mood.
What are you favourite brands?
   Bottega Veneta, Isabel Marant, Jil Sander, Prada.
What's an emerging French brand we should look out for?
   Françoise.

What's your favourite item of clothing?

My white Mango T-shirt.

What's your top tip for creating a Parisian wardrobe?

Avoid prints and regularly sort through your wardrobe to get rid of anything you haven't worn for two years. Focus on the essentials that I talked about above.

How can we follow the trends without being too much of a 'fashion victim'?

Adapt a trend without trying to reproduce the entire catwalk look.

What are your favourite places in Paris?

Vintage shops in Le Marais and the 11th arrondissement, Hotel Costes, Place de Vosges, Le Bon Marché for items for the home, the greengrocer's next to my apartment, and L'Orangerie for exhibitions.

The pillars of my Parisian capsule wardrobe: The essentials and where they came from

Despite the term 'capsule wardrobe' originally being coined by a Brit, I believe that Parisiennes have truly mastered the art of a pared-back wardrobe: an artfully put-together *armoire*, carefully curated with pieces that they love – items that are all perfectly in sync and can be coordinated with each other. Versatility is key with wardrobe essentials, so the items here can be mixed and matched. Ultimately, a capsule wardrobe is full of items that you can't wait to wear again (and that bring you joy, Marie Kondo-style), and where there is space in between the hangers. And when I say Parisian, I'm talking about timeless pieces. But don't worry, I'm not just going to tell you to buy a blue-and-white striped top. That would be a little too easy (although they do undoubtedly look good with jeans or cropped beige trousers, so you should indeed own one, ideally purchased from a classic French brand, such as Saint James or Petit Bateau). Rather, the idea of this section is to give you an outline of my key wardrobe items and where they came from, to guide you and help you banish that dreaded 'I have nothing to wear' feeling once and for all.

The derrière-enhancing jean

I've always associated denim with the US, thanks to American cowboys, Levi's, Bruce Springsteen in *those* budgie-smuggling blue wash jeans, an eighties Whitney Houston and, of course, Madonna – specifically in her video for 'Papa Don't Preach'. When researching this book, however, I was surprised to discover that denim actually originates from Nimes, France. The word 'denim' comes from the French '*serge de Nimes*'. *Serge* means 'a sturdy fabric', so 'denim' quite literally means 'from Nimes'(*de Nimes*). Nimes was once home to a thriving textile industry, and its inhabitants would dye wool, silk and cotton in the river that runs through the city. In the 1860s, businessman Levi Strauss discovered the material and exported it by the boatload to the United States, christening his new-found, soon-to-be-world-famous fabric 'denim'.

When I think about the one item that I wear every day, that my most stylish influencer and fashion editor friends wear more than anything else, it is a good pair of jeans. Nobody does the jean and blazer ensemble better than the Parisiennes, and, as I stated earlier, there is perhaps no outfit more identifiably Parisian than the white-shirt-and-jeans combo. My own denim story has been a long one – it started in my childhood, when my dad used to buy me pairs of jeans from GAP – but it's in Paris where I perfected the look.

Go-to brands: Citizens of Humanity, Goldsign, Agolde, J Brand, Rouje, GAP, Arket, Sézane, Levi's, Frame, RE/DONE, L'Agence and Mother.

⚜

The perfect pair of derrière-enhancing jeans – and how to style them

My jeans are one of the most important items in my wardrobe since I moved to Paris, and you'll notice that a good pair of jeans is the piece of clothing that pops up the most in the interviews throughout this section. I often get asked how to find the perfect jean style, and I give the same answer every time, as I believe I've found the most flattering style, and one that is likely to suit the majority of female bodies. That style is a straight-legged, high-waisted jean that falls just above the ankle. It will balance out larger hips (if you have them) and elongate your legs, while the high waist will enhance your middle as well as your behind, helping to create that 'peachy' silhouette many of us are aiming for.

Tried-and-tested jean formulas
— Jeans + white shirt (see page 67) + black bra
    + loafers (Tods, Prada, ATP Atelier, Hereu,
    Russell & Bromley) or plimsolls (Supergas, Veja,

Converse) – a classic Parisian combo (and one that doesn't date)

— Jeans + fashion top – think a silk top with billowing sleeves by the likes of Orseund Iris or Ganni

— Jeans + T-shirt + oversized blazer (see below) + sock boots (see page 68) or a block-heel sandal/ mule (Rouje, By Far, Aeyde, Miista) – accessorise with a leather belt and layer necklaces over the T-shirt

— Jeans + body (Everlane, Agolde, Jacquemus, Sézane) or 'going out' top (ROTATE Birger Christensen, Rixo, Reformation) + blazer (see below) thrown over as a cover up

— Jeans + twin set (cardigan and top – Khaite, COS) + trench (see page 66)

The blazer

Besides a good pair of jeans, no item works harder in my wardrobe than a black blazer. I wear it with jeans, over dresses, with skirts and layered with jumpers. More recently, I wore it to a wedding reception in the evening when the temperature dropped. Although I associate this piece with Paris, the blazer first appeared in the pages of *Vogue* in 1893 and is thought to have originated in St John's College, Cambridge, in the 1820s where it was first worn by a boating team. By the early twentieth century, it was a staple in many women's wardrobes.

Over time, its style has morphed and changed, but it has never gone out of fashion. It has been reinvented many times over. In the eighties, the blazer was reborn with big shoulders and became an integral piece of the 'power suit' movement that accompanied women into the boardroom. A looser, more relaxed version was worn by Princess Diana in the nineties. In Paris, the iconic blazer is black. I like to think of it as the granddaughter of Yves Saint Laurent's *'Le Smoking'* suit, after it divorced from the trousers. Today, the style is slightly oversized, butt-skimming and with some light padding in the shoulders, rather like you're wearing your boyfriend's suit jacket.

Go-to brands: Arket, The Frankie Shop, House of Dagmar, Le 17 Septembre, Musier, Acne Studios, Joseph

The tuxedo: 'Le Smoking'

As I've explained, *'Le Smoking'* is an iconic tuxedo suit for women created by Yves Saint Laurent in 1966 for his autumn/winter collection. The style not only became a seminal Parisian outfit, but also an iconic fashion ensemble. In the podcast *Habitudes*, created by French menswear magazine, *L'Etiquette*, Jane Birkin states that there is nothing better than *'Le Smoking'* for every occasion: *'Si vous avez ça dans votre armoire, ça et un chemisier par Agnès B en soie – ça avec un smoking – vous pouvais aller par tout.'* ('If you have that in your wardrobe, and a silk blouse by Agnès B., you can go anywhere'.) *'Le Smoking'* introduced a new way of dressing for a generation of women who weren't afraid to reveal their masculine side, and also wanted to try and close the equality gap between men and women. And I think a woman wearing a suit can be very sexy – just look at Anne-Laure Mais in suit pants, or Alice Barbier, one half of @jaimetoutcheztoi on Instagram.

Go-to brands: House of Dagmar, Vince, Sézane, Sandro, The Frankie Shop

The trench coat

Another item that originated from – you might have guessed it – Britain, yet one that has become synonymous with Parisian style, is the beige trench. (I have at least three in my wardrobe.) There are various contradicting stories about how the trench we know, love and wear today first came to be, but the one that I've found on

repeat is that it was first introduced by Scottish chemist and inventor Charles Macintosh (hence its name 'Mac' in the UK) and English inventor Thomas Hancock, who founded the rubber industry in Britain in the 1820s. It was then adapted by both Aquascutum and Burberry. Although they still battle it out for the claim to legitimacy, both had a hand in the coat's evolution, and in the sixties it began making frequent cameos in the movie industry. In the US, it was donned by Audrey Hepburn in *Breakfast at Tiffany's*, and in France it was elevated to iconic status through movies such as the 1967 *Love on a Pillow* starring Brigitte Bardot, who wears the classic beige style in what looks like a wool and cashmere mix. Then there's Catherine Deneuve's sexed-up patent black version in *Belle du Jour.* Both the beige trench and its sexier style are refashioned yearly by designers. If you're looking to invest in a Parisian essential that won't go out of fashion, you can't go wrong with the trench.

Go-to brands: Totême, A. P. C., House of Dagmar, The Frankie Shop, Les Coyotes de Paris, le.apt

The white shirt

A white, crisp yet comfortable and slightly oversized shirt will see you through every eventuality and occasion, as mine does me. It is one of the most versatile pieces of clothing ever to have been invented. It can be dressed up or dressed down, and you can wear it in winter under warmer layers or over a swimsuit on holiday to protect your skin from the sun. The first known 'modern day' version was worn by Marie Antoinette, who shocked society by posing in a simple frilly collared white blouse with billowing sleeves that resembled the period's undergarments, rather than in her usual outfits made from the finest silks, which were considered more becoming attire for a queen. Despite its initial shock factor, the portrait, painted by Madame Vigée Le Brun, sparked an uplift in the cotton trade (and consequently, sadly, the slave trade). The garment eventually evolved into the simple white cotton shirt we wear and love today.

Thanks to Chanel, who was transforming the way women dressed in the thirties – (often by borrowing from the boys), the white shirt became a wardrobe staple for women wanting to feel comfortable yet elegant. And like its equally wearable cousin, the trench, movies of the 1940s helped propel it into the public's consciousness. Everyone from Marlene Dietrich to Audrey Hepburn wore white shirts, both on and off camera. The fact that it has been refashioned so many times over,  by brands old and new, is testament to its wearability and iconic wardrobe status. The white shirt was also an integral item in the Celine woman's wardrobe when Phoebe Philo held the iconic brand's reins.

Go-to brands: Citizens of Humanity, Jacquemus, Anine Bing, Uniqlo, Gant, Equipment, Marie Marot

The low-heeled sock boot

As I explained earlier in the chapter, not only are the Paris streets impractical for higher heels, but my fellow

Parisiennes prefer comfort over tottering around on potential ankle-breakers. One of the most-worn shoes, and the main style in Rouje's shoe collection for example, is the low-heeled sock boot. It is both easy to wear and comfy, and at the same time oozes elegance. Tight round the ankle so that it can be worn neatly under jeans and trousers, it looks just as good on a naked leg, as the leather perfectly envelops the ankle.

Go-to brands: By Far, Loq, Rouje, Miista, Acne Studios

The basket bag

The basket bag most recently made a comeback thanks to the LOEWE leather-trimmed version (one of my star summer buys of the last two years). This was swiftly followed by an interpretation from French fashion darling Simon Porte Jacquemus, who designed it with his signature pops of colour. Although basket-weaving dates back to Egyptian times, basket bags first became a fashion item in the 1960s, according to London fashion curator Shonagh Marshall. Basket bags were synonymous with holidays and being well-off, since they were generally only available in seaside destinations, and therefore bought by those who could afford to travel. They gained iconic status when Jane Birkin began carrying one in the sixties. Ironically, they are now among the least pricey bag styles out there, and can be picked up at a market for around 20 euros. The French fashion designer Vanessa Seward once called the basket bag the 'anti-it bag' as it 'showed taste over money'. Although there are plenty of luxury options, a basket bag doesn't need to be expensive to look elegant.

Go-to brands: LOEWE, Sézane, Jacquemus, A.P.C., Chloé, Celine

The cardigan

I love the cardigan for its versatility and warmth. Known as the *gilet* in French, the cardigan had its not-so-humble beginnings in Britain. It was named after the seventh Earl of Cardigan, James Brudenell. He was a British Army Major General who led the Charge of the Light Brigade at the Battle of Balaclava during the Crimean War. The cardigan as we know it today is based on a knitted wool waistcoat worn by British officers during the war. In the US, women began wearing the cardigan (or 'sloppy joe', as it was known in East-coast colleges at the time) in the 1940s. According to Deirdre Clemente, a historian of twentieth-century fashion, their choice to wear them was a sign of their refusal to adhere to a concept of prescribed femininity. 'They began to wear Sloppy Joes around the same time they started to wear pants,' says Clemente. It was also a rebellion against restrictions in society, including the girdle that was designed to sculpt the female body.

The cardigan arrived in Paris (a city that knows all

too well what it means to revolt) in the seventies, and *maisons* such as Kenzo and Chloé reinterpreted it for a new age, giving it iconic fashion status.

The twinset has also recently been given a new lease of life following New York brand Khaite's bra-and-cardigan combo, famously worn by Katie Holmes (every high-street brand has since created a version), and updated most recently by one of Paris's most followed influencers, Sabina Socol, in her collaboration with London-based knitwear label b.Fleurs – because who better to create a capsule cardigan collection than a Parisienne?! It's a staple collection piece that is updated every season by Parisian brands Sézane and Rouje. Needless to say, you should have a cardigan in your closet. Tip: chose a wool/alpaca blend for extra cosiness.

Go to brands: Claudie Pierlot, Eric Bompard, Vince, Sézane, Rouje, b.Fleurs, Lou Lou Studio

The 'wear with everything' bag

In my opinion, this bag could be one of two different designs, the 'baguette' or a small cross-body bag.

The 'baguette' – This is an iconic style that was launched in the nineties by Fendi and worn by the likes of Sarah Jessica Parker in *Sex in the City* (who, incidentally, featured in Fendi's ad campaign to promote their upgraded style, released in 2019). It's a small, structured bag, with a short handle that's meant to tuck neatly under the shoulder of the wearer. The 'baguette' has since become synonymous with style, French elegance and the concept of what an everyday bag should look like. There have been numerous takes on it in recent years, from Coperni's 'Sac Swipe' to Prada's most recent offering – the 'Cleo'.

Go-to brands: Little Liffner, Coperni, Prada, By Far, Elleme, Manu Atelier, Nico Giani, Simon Miller

A small crossbody bag – This is the style that I personally wear every day. I would advise choosing one in navy or black, with minimal hardware – gold is better. Think Celine's 'Trotteur' or 'Classic Bag' or Hermès 'Constance' bag. And it should be made from good-quality Italian leather, so that it will last. Better yet, go for a patent mock-croc or lizard motif, as this will help hide any scratching and later wear and tear. I personally also love A. P. C.'s 'half-moon' design, which has become an iconic French style.

Go-to brands: Leo + Violette, A. P. C., LOEWE, Sézane, Celine, Chloe, Hermès, ATP Atelier, Chylak, Polène Paris, Wicker Wings, Mulberry

The one-piece swimming costume

While a swimming costume isn't an everyday piece, I think it's important to include it in my Parisian wardrobe essentials as it's the main swimwear style I wear every summer. Also, because of its design, it can be worn as a body with shorts or a skirt – and as we've learned, a key aspect of the Parisian wardrobe is versatility. If there is one swimwear style that a Parisienne is sure to have in her wardrobe it's a one-piece swimming costume. They are no longer associated with the sporty styles worn by professional swimmers. The famous designs – streamlined silhouettes that mould to the body – really do wonders for the figure, flattering you in all the right places, and the Parisienne's go-to brand is Eres (see page 85).

Go-to brands: Eres (obviously), Hunza G, Rouje, Sézane, Solid & Striped, YSE, Evarae, Peony, Ernest Leoty, Magda Butrym

A style chat with Anne-Laure Mais

Anne-Laure (@annelauremais) is one of France's most followed fashion influencers, with 634,000 followers and counting. She's a fixture at Fashion Weeks and regularly features on sites like Who What Wear as a French girl to follow. She launched her own brand, Musier, in 2018.

How would you define your style?

Feminine and comfortable.

And how would you describe Parisian style?

Effortless.

What are your Parisian wardrobe essentials?

A masculine oversized blazer in wool, a vintage pair of Levi's 501 jeans, a pair of leather boots with a comfortable heel, an everyday bag and a navy blue jumper.

And your tip for dressing a little more Parisian without looking too clichéd?

Don't make too much effort – that's the most important.

What or who inspires your clothing choices?

I go by instinct, but always make comfort a priority.

What are your favourite brands?

Jacquemus, Nodaleto, Marcia, Musier, Redone, Christopher Esber. And I'm obsessed by vintage Prada, Dior and Chanel.

What's your favourite item of clothing?

My vintage Levi's 501 jeans, which I wear every day.

What are your favourite places in Paris?

My favourite restaurants are Kitchen Garden, Aux Près de Cyril Lignac, Apicius. My favourite shops include Galeries Lafayette Champs Elysées.

❧

Parisian capsule wardrobe seasonal shopping lists

When creating a Parisian capsule wardrobe, always keep these things in mind: pare back, invest, keep treasures and heirlooms, and seek out vintage finds, but here's my seasonal shopping list to help you create a capsule wardrobe.

Autumn/winter
— Slightly oversized black blazer (see page 64)
— White shirt (see page 67)
— A good fitting bodysuit – Everlane, Agolde, Alix, Sézane
— Straight-legged/slightly flared jeans (see page 62)
— Loafers
— Leather jacket – Acne Studios, Anine Bing
— Cardigan (see page 70)
— Midi slip skirt – Rixo, Vince, House of Dagmar, & Other Stories
— Sock boots (see page 68)

— Tailored, high-waisted wool trousers – The Frankie Shop, Vince, House of Dagmar, Lemaire, Joseph
— Wrap coat/dressing-gown coat – COS, Maxmara, & Other Stories
— Puffer coat – Nanushka, Totême, ienki ienki, LU MEI
— Tuxedo Suit/*'Le Smoking'* (see page 65)
— 'Going out' top – Ganni, Rixo, ROTATE, Nensi Dojaka, Khaite, Magda Butrym
— Cashmere knit – Vince, Eric Bompard, Tricot, Notshy
— Sneakers or Dad Trainers – New Balance, Adidas, Veja, Acne Studios

Spring/summer
— Basket bag (see page 69)
— Wrap dress/floral dress – Rixo, Dôen, Rouje, Kitri, Musier, Mirae Paris
— Little black dress/white dress – Tove, Jacquemus, & Other Stories
— Espadrilles – Castana, Rouje, Sézane
— Trench (see page 66)
— Block-heeled sandals – By Far, Loq, Ayede
— White/ecru jeans – Agolde, & Other Stories
— Flat sandals – ATP Atelier, Chanel, Hermès
— Linen blazer – Arket, House of Dagmar
— Barely-there sandals – Row, Arket
— Plimsolls – Supergas, Converse
— Denim jacket – Goldsign, Anine Bing, Levi's

✤

My top tip for investment buys

Create wish lists with all your favourite online retailers (mine are Net-a-Porter, Matches, Farfetch, MyTheresa, 24S and Printemps). When the sales start, keep a beady eye on these items and, if you're clever, you can catch them at as much as 80 per cent off. They won't be current season of course, but investment buys should be timeless items that transcend the seasons. For example, I might invest in a couple of dresses for summer and a pair of sandals that I know I'll wear for years to come.

✤

My go-to brands for:

Elevated basics
— Line by K, Totême, Arket, House of Dagmar,
   The Frankie Shop, Deveaux, Tove, COS, Vince

Fun, more colourful and fashion-forward items
— Ganni, Rouje, Nanushka, Rejina Pyo, Rixo, Kitri,
   Musier, Cult Gaia, Acne Studios

Shoes
— ATP Atelier, By Far, Ayede

A style chat with Ellie Delphine

Ellie (@slipintostyle) is a fashion influencer. I love her look, which is perhaps a little ironic, because it is so different to what I would describe as 'classically' Parisian. And yet, precisely because it's colourful, loud and rule-breaking, it is at the same time *very* Parisian: Ellie dresses undeniably for herself, and her clothing choices truly match her opinions. She is one of the most outspoken fashion influencers on social issues, and a rare breed whereby her clothes do not drown out her voice – they complement it.

How would you describe your style?
My style is colourful, eclectic, sometimes experimental but definitely fun.

How would you describe Parisian style and fashion?
Parisian style is chic, classic, but a bit too safe for my taste.

Your style is notoriously colourful, which is what makes it quite unique in a city like Paris – who or what inspires your clothing choices?
I was born in the Caribbean, so I grew up surrounded by the beautiful colours of bountiful nature. When I moved to Paris and saw that everybody was wearing mostly black, it quite depressed me, so I decided to stay true to my roots and wear colour as often as possible for my own mental health. I find

colour inspiration everywhere I go: in flowers at the park, in paintings at the museum... ˎ

What are your go-to brands for fashion?

I love Ganni for their quirky and colourful prints and designs, and The Frankie Shop for minimal and casual pieces.

What's your favourite item of clothing?

Right now, jogger pants. They're the only thing I wear, because they're comfy and versatile. I wear them with boots if I'm in the mood for a masculine look, with high-heeled pumps if I'm feeling dressier, and with sneakers when I'm out and about or running errands.

What are your wardrobe essentials?

A good pair of sneakers, a good pair of jeans and a more formal blazer that you can throw on over any outfit – I like mine slightly oversized.

What are your tips for finding your own style?

I would say go for what you like, for what suits your figure and stick to it. You may want to look for inspiration in magazines and on Instagram, but do not let anyone else dictate your style. Dress for your own joy.

What are your 3 favourite places in Paris?

I love going to Sunday brunch at Nomad's, then to Jardin des Tuileries on a sunny day. I sit by the fountain on a lounge chair, watch the ducks and work on my tan.

My favourite museums are the Musée Bourdelle – it's incredibly peaceful and quiet – and the Musée Jacquemart André, for its beautiful, richly decorated rooms. As for restaurants, Brasserie Baroche has been a go-to for many years: the owner is hilarious, and the food never disappoints.

A note on jewellery and how to wear it

Another item that is crucial to my wardrobe – and those of my fellow Parisiennes – is jewellery. In an interview with *French Vogue*, Paris-born, London-based jewellery and ceramics designer, Anissa Kermiche (who I'll return to later in the Interiors & Home Life chapter) said: 'Parisian girls usually opt for the more delicate pieces, understated diamond rings, mini hoop earrings, all very subtle. London girls have bolder taste, choosing the more "statement" pieces like the large earrings – she generally has more piercings – and chunky rings. Their goal is to be seen, eccentricity and individuality are more accepted here. The Parisian, on the other hand, will wear more pared-back pieces where it's the small details that count – less is more for a French girl.'

On the whole, understated, dainty pieces of jewellery are indeed preferred to large statement items, although a short, chunky necklace will look good layered over a white T-shirt or paired with a shirt, for example. Just keep the rest of your jewellery to a minimum.

Go-to brands: Missoma, Anissa Kermiche, Aligieri, Louise Damas, Maison Chaumet (for high-end investment pieces), Maria Black

✦ **TOP TIP** ✦
Invest in sterling silver, gold-plated silver or solid gold jewellery.

A conversation about Parisian style with Monica de La Villardière

Monica (@monicaainleydlv) is a fellow expat, originally from Canada. She reports on fashion for Elle.fr, contributes regularly to British Vogue, and, together with Camille Charrière, she hosts *Fashion no Filter*, a podcast that dissects fashion. After studying French and then journalism in Edinburgh and London, Monica moved to Paris five years ago. She lives in the 6th arrondissement with her Parisian husband.

What is it about Parisian style that makes it so iconic?
There's a uniform, there's a lot of neutral colours, and a lot of figuring out what shapes look good on you – and not getting bored of wearing them. I would say it's not that there is no accessorising or colour, it's just that they indulge in them with a certain amount of restraint.

So they're just really good at paring back/curating their lives?
Yes. You have an embarrassing amount *du choix* in Paris. You have the most beautiful food and fashion available to you (if you have the money) and because they have all of that at their fingertips from a very, very young age, they just don't get overwhelmed by it. I think [curation] is their forte. I even see my husband doing this. There are no two pieces in his wardrobe that you could not wear together. He dresses very simply, but it's also stylish. As the seasons change and the years develop, he might add maybe one A. P. C. jacket. He's not

buying clothes the whole time. The women are, to a certain extent, very similar – maybe they will buy a few more pieces.

Parisians are not constantly reinventing themselves. They allow certain indulgences, but few and far between. And they invest in quality pieces that will last for a long time, rather than bingeing.

There's an expression I love that I learned from my husband (who has said it to me several times): *'Tu te noies dans un verre d'eau'* – which means, 'You're drowning yourself in a glass of water'. (In other words, you're really over-thinking this.) That's a big part of their philosophy. In terms of fashion, the last thing you want to look like is that you made too much of an effort, it's just a no-go!

What would every Parisian woman, in your opinion, have in her wardrobe?

I think she would have a pair of jeans that really look good on her. And then she'd wear them for years and really work them in. There's a lot of vintage Levi's in that equation. She would have a couple of great blazers, a selection of T-shirts (but not zillions of them) – white T-shirts, shirts, collared button-down shirts. She would have a great coat. Then she'd have the right pair of *bottines* (boots) – she would probably have a flat pair and a heeled pair. Parisian women don't dress in an overtly sexy way, but the style is very sexy and very nonchalant.

What are your favourite French brands?

Chanel, Hermès, Louis Vuitton, Michel Vivien, Pierre Hardy, Admise Paris, Loulou Studio Paris, A. P. C.

What's an up-and-coming Parisian brand you love?

Viltier – the most beautiful fine jewellery, with a very modern point of view.

What are your favourite places in Paris?

Brasserie Lipp for wine with friends, Cafe de La Poste for lunch, the secret garden at Hotel de L'Abbaye for a summer *apéro*. And, in my humble opinion, no physical shopping experience can ever beat Le Bon Marché Rive Gauche!

❖

ADDRESS BOOK

Bricks-and-mortar shops to visit

A. P. C. (multiple locations)

L'Appartement Sézane *(www.sezane.com*
   – 1 Rue Saint-Fiacre, 75002)

ba&sh (multiple locations)

Le Bon Marché *(www.24sevres.com*
   – 24 Rue de Sèvres, 75007)

Centre Commercial *(www.centrecommerical.cc*
   – 2 Rue de Marseille, 75010)

Elleme *(www.elleme.com*
   – 19 Rue Ferdinand Duval, 75004)

Eric Bompard (multiple locations)

The Frankie Shop *(www.thefrankieshop.com*
  – 14 Rue Saint-Claude, 75003)
French Trotters *(www.frenchtrotters.fr*
  – 128 Rue Vieille du Temple, 75003)
Galeries Lafayette *(galererieslafayette.com*
  – multiple locations)
Leo et Violette *(www.leoetviolette.com*
  – 12 Rue Sainte-Anne, 75001)
Merci *(www.merci.com*
  – 111 Boulevard Beaumarchais, 75003)
Passage Dore (sells Louise Damas jewellery)
  (passagedore.com – 6 Rue du Château d'Eau,
  75010)
Printemps *(printemps.com – multiple locations)*
Rouje *(www.rouje.com*
  – 11 bis, Rue Bachaumont, 75002)
RSVP *(www.rsvp-paris.com*
  – 133 Rue Vieille du Temple, 75003)
La Samaritaine *9 Rue de la Monnaie, 75001*

Lingerie and swimwear
Eres *(www.eresparis.com – multiple locations)*
Yasmine Eslami *(www.yasmine-eslami.com*
  – 35 Rue de Richelieu, 75001)
Ysé *(www.yse-paris.com – multiple locations)*

Online addresses
Coperni *(www.coperniparis.com)*
Francoise *(francoise-paris.com)*
Jacquemus *(www.jacquemus.com)*

Marcia *www.marciawear.com*
Marie Marot *(www.mariemarot.com)*
Marine Serre *(marineserre.com)*
Mirae *(www.miraeparis.com)*
Musier *(musier-paris.com)*
Notshy *(www.notshy.fr)*
Officine Générale *(www.officinegenerale.com)*

Vintage:
Bonsergent Studio *(www.bonsergent-studio.com*
   – online only)
Kiliwatch *(www.kiliwatch.paris*
   – 64 Rue Tiquetonne, 75002)
Kilo Shop *(www.kiloshop.com – multiple locations)*
Rose Market Vintage *(www.rosemarketvintage.com*
   – 19 Rue Milton, 75009)
Thanx God I'm a V.I.P. *(www.thanxgod.com*
   – 12 Rue de Lancry, 75010)
The Hippy Market *(www.hippymarket.com*
   – 41 Rue du Temple, 75004)
Vintage Clothing Paris *(www.vintageclothingparis.com*
   – 10 Rue de Crussol, 75011)
Vintage Désir *(32 Rue des Rosiers, 75004)*

Beauty, skincare, body image & wellbeing

An au naturel approach

*'In each country, I think there is an idea of what beauty is
... For the French, it's very particular: what we want is to
be ourselves – not a better version of ourselves. We feel like
it's better to be used to something than to try to change it.
So we think: what style can I have with this face, and with
this hair? That mentality is 100 per cent French'*

Violette, French make-up artist and founder of VIOLETTE_FR

I believe Parisians have a very different – and very positive – approach to beauty, and that's another reason
why I've written this book. I think there's so much we
can learn from our cousins across the Channel about
make-up, skincare, wellbeing and, most importantly, the
relationship we have with our appearance and bodies. In
Paris, women generally wear less make-up; they champion natural beauty, are less likely to go under the knife
in order to preserve their youth, are less afraid
of growing older, and rarely diet. Exercise is
something to do to stay healthy, not
to obsess over. They follow a more
relaxed and 'effortless' approach
– yes, there's that word again,
but it really does encapsulate a
Parisienne's outlook on life. As

Charlotte Morel, co-founder of art house We Do Not Work Alone, states: 'A Parisian can go out without styling her hair, without a manicure, sit without crossing her legs. Our laidback attitude doesn't exist anywhere else.'

As in many other areas of their lives, less is considered more when it comes to a Parisienne's make-up and beauty routine. In the years that I have lived here, I have learned a lot about beauty, skincare and how to make the most of my body from my fellow Parisiennes, and have, as such, adapted the way I look after my skin, how I do my make-up and how I view my body. One of the many things I love about Parisian skincare and beauty brands is that some of the stories behind the brands are just as enchanting as the products themselves. Take the inspiration for EviDenS de Beauté, for example, which is one of the best anti-ageing brands on the market, specialising in products for sensitive skin. The Franco-Japanese brand was born out of the love that the French founder, Charles-Edouard Barthes, had for his Japanese wife. After observing her skincare routine and admiring the way she cared for her skin, he decided to create a brand that paid homage to her beauty and married art with technology.

Since moving to Paris, I have discovered the merits (and magical powers) of micellar water, a make-up removing miracle that every Parisienne is sure to have tucked away in her bathroom cabinet. I know how to apply lipstick so that my lips have that 'just been kissed' look; I know that great skincare doesn't have to be expensive; and I have stopped caring about my boobs – or lack thereof. My perception of beauty has also changed. I no longer subscribe to the more 'Hollywood' ideal that I grew up with in the UK. Although this ideal is gradually changing, thanks to the likes of Alicia Keys, who 'shocked' the media when she started going make-up-free in 2016, it still dominates, promoting an air of faux perfection, with a lot of focus on make-up, quick fixes and Botox. You only have to watch a few of those appalling contouring videos on YouTube to know what I'm talking about. And to return to the quote I shared at the beginning of the section: above all, Parisians want to be themselves. They don't want to hide the way they look under layers of foundation and concealer, nor do they want to drastically alter their features with plastic surgery.

There is also a very different attitude towards ageing here, and being surrounded by women who care less about it has changed my own mindset. The Parisian approach towards growing older is much healthier, and also more humorous, as they are not afraid to poke fun at it. So much so that Caroline de Maigret, author *of How to be a Parisian*, recently wrote a book about it with Sophie Mas, entitled *Older But Better, But Older*. I also admire the Parisian approach towards health, wellbeing and exercise. They might do yoga in the morning and smoke a cigarette in the evening (not that I'm advocating smoking, but you see my point). And they might sweat at the gym and then eat pizza for lunch. Life is to be enjoyed, but they just know how to show a little more restraint, which, as I mentioned in the Style & Fashion chapter, could be a hangover from the revolution, or could be to do with the fact that they live in a city surrounded by so much beauty and excess in terms of architecture that they've gone in the opposite direction in other areas of their lives.

Positivity and balance

'The coolest French girl is the girl who makes
people think she isn't trying too hard – and,
honestly, she probably isn't'
Garance Doré

As I have explained, a lot of what I believe it means to be Parisian, beyond the clichés and stereotypes, is found in their attitude: a more laidback outlook on life that also encapsulates a certain indifference towards and acceptance of one's faults. Even if they do care, they try not to show it or draw too much attention to their shortcomings. I find that Parisiennes focus less on their flaws because – and it comes down to something very simple – there are just more important things to enjoy in life. This sentiment was shared with me by a Parisian friend when we were discussing this book and her own attitude towards make-up, beauty and appearance. She was recounting how, when travelling with some American friends recently, she was amazed by the amount of products each had brought with them for a long weekend, in contrast to her own small, highly curated wash bag of essentials. And when she was talking about there being 'more important things to enjoy', I believe she was referring to the concept of *joie de vivre* that the Parisians

are so renowned for. Of course, they have their flaws –
don't be fooled into thinking that they don't – they are
just better at accepting these flaws, moving on and then
focusing their attention on more important or pleasurable
things. It's not that they are any less insecure than the rest
of us; they just have a different attitude. My friend later
pointed out the size of her bum, saying it's perhaps bigger
than she'd like, but then added that she doesn't really
care. Aiming for 'perfection' and 'living at 100 per cent',
as discussed by Pandora Sykes in her book *How Do We
Know We're Doing it Right?* is, after all, exhausting, and
Parisians prefer to lead a more leisurely and pleasurable
lifestyle. Their lives look more effortless because they are!

The value of this more positive attitude and laidback
approach can easily be seen through the way the rest
of the world views the concept of French beauty. It's
no secret that the French are revered, not only for their
appearance, but also for their positive attitude towards
beauty and skincare. There is a keen emphasis on keeping
it natural and cherishing what nature gave you, and this
is reflected in the products they use, and how often they
apply them. Many French pharmacy products have iconic
status globally, and there's even an American beauty
brand called French Girl. Anyway – all this is to say that,
for me, there is no other breed of women so celebrated for
their approach to beauty, appearance and skincare than
the Parisiennes. And for good reason!

When it comes to the concept of wellbeing and wellness, which is slowly gathering pace in Paris, with the

opening of various gyms and wellness centres over the past few years, the Parisians still maintain a more relaxed approach, as yoga practitioner and influencer Caroline Perrineau pointed out to me on page 145. They're interested in the ways in which they can bring balance into daily life, without changing it too drastically.

A brief history of French skincare

'Beauty is a weapon!'
Coco Chanel

The French, and, more importantly, the Parisiennes, are famous for knowing a lot about what to put on one's face. They are experts, having developed and refined their knowledge and expertise over hundreds of years.

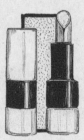 Of course, like their fashion house counterparts, French beauty companies have the advantage of having had a much longer relationship with skincare. The French interest in beauty routines and cosmetics can be dated back to the seventeenth century. According to Melanie Clegg, author of *Marie Antoinette: An Intimate History*, when King Louis XVI's grandfather first heard about his grandson's future wife, the Austrian-born Marie Antoinette, he was apparently 'appalled' by 'her poor grooming while she was still a princess in Austria, and insisted that French hairdressers and clothes be sent to her, along with a French dentist to straighten her teeth and encourage her to brush them more often'.

Although skincare and beauty have obviously come a long way since the seventeenth century, Parisians can undoubtedly be considered as pioneers of the beauty industry. Early Parisian cosmetic brands, now behemoth-sized corporate companies, were founded as far back as 1828 (Guerlain). The now American-owned, Parisian-born brand Bourjois created the first blush in 1863. There are also newer brands, such as Horace: a French men's grooming brand founded in 2016, which has been steadily gaining popularity in the UK – so much so that women happily use their products too. Incidentally, it's also in Paris where the world's first microplastic-free lipstick refill was launched by French beauty brand La Bouche Rouge. Their lipsticks are also free from parabens and silicone, and come in recyclable, stainless steel bullets: both aesthetically pleasing and better for the environment.

Talking of the environment, French beauty brands have more of a tendency to make use of their country's surrounding landscape and nature – as skincare influencer Emma Houreau points out in her interview on page 123. The French look to their natural surroundings for inspiration and ingredients. A prime example of this is Caudalie – the first skincare brand to harness the power of vines. The founder, Mathilde Thomas, grew up on her parents' winemaking estate, Château Smith Haut-Lafitte in Bordeaux in southwest France. During their harvest in 1993, a chance meeting with Professor Joseph Vercauteren, the laboratory director of the Pharmacy University of Bordeaux, sparked a life-changing idea. He told them that the grape seeds contain the most powerful anti-oxidants in the world. In 1995, at the age of twenty-three, Mathilde and her now-husband and co-founder, Bertrand, set out to show pharmacists the three products that they'd created using grape seed polyphenols in the two years following their encounter with Vercauteren. The rest, as they say is history, and Caudalie is now one of the largest skincare companies in the world.

Another example of this, is the Parisian-born, self-dubbed 'high-performance botanical skincare brand', Darphin. Inspired by French queens, namely Marie Antoinette, who developed a penchant for the properties of orange blossom during her time as queen of France, Pierre Darphin, a master botanist and kinesiotherapist made it his mission to harness the power of plants and their essences to create formulas for the skin. Darphin founded the brand in 1958, and today it's a major player in the skincare market. Meanwhile, when it comes to perfume, the region of Grasse in the south of France has been cultivating flowers for perfume since the fourteenth century.

My skincare story

'Beauty begins the moment you decide to be yourself'
Coco Chanel

I've always taken good care of my skin, but this is something that was instilled in me from a young age by my mother, who, perhaps unusually for the era that I grew up in, always paid a lot of attention to hers. She had learned the hard way, after burning her face so badly while living in Kenya in the seventies that her skin blistered. Growing up, I remember her forgoing other luxuries in favour of expensive night creams, eye creams and foundation, and today she will often send me article clippings or photos of new products she's read about. It was my mum who introduced me to the likes of Estée Lauder's Advanced Night Repair and Elizabeth Arden's Eight Hour Cream, two products that remain essential to my skincare routine. By the age of twelve, I was using the three-step Clinique routine of cleanser, toner and moisturiser. I knew early on the difference between good and bad skincare products, but contrary to what I have since learned while living in Paris, I had always thought that great skincare products equalled expensive. Of course, lower-cost brands such as The Ordinary now exist, but it was in Paris where affordable and effective skincare products were first readily available, hence why French pharmacy products have gained such an iconic status outside of France. It's also worth pointing out that one of the UK's front-running beauty and skincare influencers, Emma Hoareau (interviewed on page 123) is half French, and spent her childhood living in Paris. Although she is now based in London, I wanted to talk to her for this section, as her approach to skincare and body image perfectly encapsulates a Parisienne's attitude towards beauty.

Parisian beauty is perfectly imperfect

'I love everything that's a little blurry. I'm not looking for perfection, on the contrary'

Jeanne Damas

It feels like it's rare for a week to go by without some publication or website touting the merits of French skin-care or offering tips on how to dress in a way that's a little more Parisian. Thanks to this attitude, the Parisians have picked up a reputation for being somewhat 'perfect' in everything that they do. And I, of course, play my own part in fuelling this idea, when I champion their aesthetics or sense of style in the articles I've written for Who What Wear and in the images I show on my Instagram. But I would argue (and I'm probably not the first to say this) that what makes them so influential (and aspirational), is in fact the opposite: their enviable approach towards beauty lies not in its perfection, but in its imperfection. The above quote comes from a short video promoting Rouje's make-up by the brand's founder, Parisian it-girl Jeanne Damas, who, for many, is the modern epitome of la Parisienne. She has naturally coloured hair, a small fringe, wears minimal make-up (just a flick of mascara and some slightly smudged red lipstick) and usually wears high-waisted, straight-legged jeans, ankle sock boots and vintage-inspired cardigans, while carrying a basket bag. For me, her statement perfectly sums up a Parisian's attitude towards looks and appearance, as it echoes the 'effortlessness' that is so intrinsic to a Parisian's way of life. Put less pressure on 'perfect' and more emphasis on pleasure! I think this philosophy towards everything from fashion and style to skincare is why so many of us seek to emulate Parisian methods.

And so, like in every section of this book, I will talk about my own experiences and the lessons I've learned about make-up, skincare, body care, exercise, health, diet and nutrition thanks to my Parisian friends. I will be turning my magnifying glass on the products and brands that have made a name for themselves, as well as talking to experts and influencers, including skin influencer and photographer Emma Hoareau; founder of Oh My Cream, Juliette Levy; yoga practitioner Caroline Perrineau; plastic surgeon Dr Oren Marco; wellbeing journalist and Pilates instructor Julie Pujols; and founder of Holidermie, Melanie Huynh. These are all women (and men) who I think are paving the way towards a healthier, more balanced perspective on everything to do with beauty, skincare and wellbeing. I will also include my own beauty, skincare and haircare essentials, as well as tips to help you adopt a more Parisian approach in your own bathroom.

Lessons I picked up from the Parisiennes about skincare & beauty

'In France, we're more ruled by the pleasure principle. It informs everything we do, but especially beauty'
Mathilde Thomas, founder of Caudalie

As I've already mentioned, I had a pretty good introduction to skincare from my mum while I was growing up, but it's been in Paris where I've learned my most important lessons – partly because I've been more exposed to beauty and skincare products through the work that I do, but also because Paris is home to many of the world's most famous brands, so skincare and beauty just feels far more present in my day-to-day life here. While I've picked up a wealth of information and numerous tips since living in Paris, these are my most important lessons.

Good skincare doesn't have to be expensive

As I've mentioned, my mum always had expensive skincare products when I was growing up, and because of this I'd always associated good skincare with high prices.

There's a tendency to think that the more expensive a product is, the better it must be. This does ring true in some cases, but the French have proved that skincare doesn't need to be pricey to be effective. And there's a reason why French pharmacy products have star status – it's because they really are good, yet affordable. You just have to walk off the street into any pharmacy and you'll find a range of good-quality, reasonably priced products from household names including Avène, La Roche-Posay, Caudalie and Vichy. A few of my current favourite products are the beauty essentials created by newish beauty kid on the block, Oh My Cream, which includes a daily SPF moisturiser and serum. (The brand's founder, Juliette Levy, will be revealing her skincare routine on page 121.)

Less is, of course, always more

While there are a lot of brilliant brands and products on the market, the point is not to keep changing your routine, or to pile them all on your face at once. The more make-up you layer on, for example, the more clogged your pores will become, meaning your skin will need more care, and you'll probably find yourself using even more skincare products – it's a vicious cycle. Make-up such as heavy foundation can be very drying, and if you're putting powder on top, your skin won't be able to breathe. Plus, one needs to be careful when changing face creams, as I've learned the hard way a few times, with my skin breaking out immediately after testing different products

that I get sent. (Your skin cells naturally renew themselves after twenty-eight days, so this is how long you
should allow before testing out a new product.)

Foundation is for younger women

This brings me nicely on to my next lesson. Since moving
to Paris, I've learned to wear a lot less foundation. Parisiennes wear make-up to enhance their looks, not hide
them, so heavy foundation doesn't slot in well with their
aesthetics. They might only wear it on a night out or to an
important event, but even then, they prefer tinted moisturiser, a little concealer, blush, lip balm (or red lipstick
in the evening) and mascara to highlight their features,
rather than putting on layers and layers of make-up.
Another top tip: if you are pushing forty, foundation or
lots of under-eye concealer might not always be a good
choice – as you get older, the products start to cake inside
the crevices and wrinkles under your eyes and around
your mouth, actually making you look older than you are.
If you do liking wearing a thicker foundation, make sure
you drink plenty of water to keep your skin hydrated.

Red wine can be good for the skin
(in moderation, of course!)

There is another, less widely advertised reason why French
women have such great skin (in my opinion): it's because
they drink a lot of good red wine. Having grown up in a

wine-producing country where wine is the second largest export, they naturally know a little more about how to choose a good bottle of red – and, of course, good wine is more readily available. Red wine is packed full of anti-oxidants, which are anti-inflammatory, cell-restoring and even help your skin produce collagen – knowledge that Mathilde Thomas, who I mentioned on page 98, harnessed to create her successful brand. Her use of grape extracts in her Caudalie skincare range, with visible results, proves that wine consumed in the right way (in moderation, accompanied by food, or by using cleverly formulated skincare products) can actually be good for you!

Do not dye your hair a different colour, you will regret it

You have been warned. Leave it as nature intended and instead enhance your natural hue with a few highlights in summer to give it that sun-kissed look if you feel like changing things up a bit. And I speak from experience here – I'll tell you more about this later. Remaining as natural as possible is actually a very Parisian beauty characteristic, so save your hair (and your wallet) the pain, and keep it its beautiful, natural colour.

Do not apply lipstick perfectly

My mum doesn't leave the house without lipstick. She uses lip liner, then applies two layers of lipstick and finally dabs her lips with a tissue. This is her method and it works for her, but I've always thought it takes a little too much time and effort. In Paris, lipstick is applied a little differently: it's not meant to look perfect, as Jeanne Damas points out in the quote on page 101. So adopt the Rouje way and apply lipstick with fingers. It should be smudged and a little messy, for that effortless look that we are all trying to emulate. There's nothing wrong with looking like you've just been kissed – in fact, it's encouraged!

Essential skincare products in the Parisian bathroom cabinet

In the same way that they curate their wardrobes and homes, I've come to learn that there are a few key products that Parisians always have in their bathroom cabinets – often products that their mothers used, and their mothers before them. Of course they will have many more, as there are so many great brands and products available in France, but I've found the following products crop up again and again in the bathrooms of my Parisian friends, so, for me, these are the foundations of their skincare regime.

Micellar water – If there's one product that almost all my Parisian friends have in their beauty cabinets, it's micellar water by Bioderma. It's a French beauty icon, used by skincare experts and make-up artists alike.

Make-up artists will often have it as a sort of secret weapon in their beauty bag of tricks backstage at fashion shows, ready to correct a fallen blob of mascara with a cotton bud. Although it's now much more widely available, I had never even heard of micellar water when I first moved to Paris. Now I use it every day. Micellar water is hardworking, but incredibly gentle on your skin, because it doesn't contain any alcohol. In fact, it feels like you are only applying water, and it doesn't leave your skin feeling tight or oily. Use it to remove make-up, or as a gentle toner after cleansing to remove any excess dirt and oil before applying serum and cream.

My favourites: Bioderma Sensibio H2O and Chanel Micellar Cleansing Water

A high-SPF sun cream – My French friends love to tan, or at least to be a lovely brown colour during the summer. While tanning and direct sun exposure can, of course, be very dangerous, I believe a tan can be achieved safely if you know how to do it and are using the right products. For example, I wear a minimum of SPF 25 every day, even in winter and while indoors (those sunrays can get through clouds *and* windows). In summer, I wear a minimum of SPF 30, and SPF 50 when I'm on the beach, by the pool or in direct sunlight while on holiday. One of my French friends, who is of Italian origin and tans very easily to a gorgeous shade of nut-brown, always wears SPF 50 in summer (even when she is already tanned). One important piece of information to note is, the longer your skin takes to tan, the longer that tan will last. If you burn, then you'll peel – and bye bye colour. You'll also be more prone to skin cancer. So using a high-SPF sun cream will not only give you a nicer colour in the long run, it will also keep your skin healthy.

My favourite SPFs: Super Soin Solar SPF 50 by Sisley, La Roche-Posay Anthelios SPF 50, CeraVe SPF 25 Facial Moisturising Lotion, Vichy Ideal Soleil SPF 30, Kiehl's Activated Sun Protector SPF 50, Caudalie SPF 30 Milky Sun Spray and Dr Sturm SPF 50 Sun Drops

✦ TOP TIP ✦

If you don't want to tan (or can't, due to health reasons), but love being a darker colour during the summer, perhaps for aesthetic reasons, add tanning drops to your daily moisturiser – I really like 'A Hint of Summer' by Rudolf Care. They give a much more gradual and (in my opinion) natural glow. You can also take tablets to help your skin absorb the sun better, burn less and improve your colour. It's a tip I learned from my Parisian friends.

Tinted moisturiser – Tinted moisturiser has been a permanent resident of my beauty bag ever since a friend at university, who was very *au fait* with her make-up brands, introduced me to Laura Mercier. It's still one of the main tinted moisturisers that I wear today. And I've since discovered that Parisians prefer to wear a tinted moisturiser rather than a layer of foundation, as the skin will have a more natural finish and it doesn't clog pores.

> **My favourites:** Laura Mercier SPF 30 Tinted Moisturiser, Les Beiges SPF 30 by Chanel, Tinted Suncare SPF 30 by Sisley and Super Serum Skin Tint SPF 30 by Ilia

Biafine – I was first introduced to Biafine by my good friend Magali Gnocchi (who I interview in the Relationships, Love & Dating chapter), who has worked in beauty and skincare PR for many years – she's the former PR for French brand Sisley, and now runs her own agency, Belong. Biafine is a product that she takes everywhere with her, even on holiday. It's a water-based cream that was created to treat dermatitis and minor abrasions by creating an optimum environment for skin to heal. You can use it on anything from dry skin to sunburn. When I opened the drawer under the sink in my Parisian boyfriend's bathroom for the first time, low and behold, I spotted a tube in there, too.

A cream or balm cleanser – One of the reasons I think so many Parisian women have great skin, besides the fact that they are often more mindful of what they're putting into their bodies, is that they know how to take care of it, and which products to use, avoiding those that might dry it out or be abrasive to potentially sensitive skin. A cream or balm cleanser is a key ingredient in the Parisian skincare routine. These products are much gentler for your face, as they keep skin moisturised while still removing make-up and impurities. They won't dry your skin out in the way that many gels and soaps can. And what's even better is that you can use both products with a cotton pad to target areas of your face where you need to remove more make-up, or apply to dry skin and then wash off with warm water and a flannel.

My favourites: La Roche-Posay Hydrating Cleansing Cream, Cleansing Milk by Sisley, Aromatic Cleansing Balm by Darphin, the Cream Cleansing Gel with TFC8 by Augustinus Bader and Cleansing Milk by Susanne Kaufmann

Marie Gilliot's morning skincare and beauty routine

Parisian born and bred, Marie (@mariegilliot) is a model and influencer, specialising in beauty, skincare and fashion. She's a thirty-five-year-old mum of two, leads a very busy lifestyle, and has some of the best skin I've ever seen, so I asked her for her skincare and beauty routine. She says: 'One needs to know that I have sensitive and dehydrated skin. This routine functions well for my skin, but everyone is different, and it's important to use the products that work for you.'

Step 1: Cleansing Lotion by P.Lab Beauty
I don't need water in the morning or an aggressive cleanser: a lotion is enough. I apply it with a reusable cotton pad.

Step 2: Lotion P50W by Biologique Recherche
This is specially designed for sensitive skin. It's my miracle product, and I've used it for a few years now. It helps to regulate the skin and gently exfoliates. It's the end of spots and other little imperfections! I apply it by hand with tapping motions.

Step 3: Triple Hyaluronic Antioxydant Hydrating Sérum by Allies of Skin
I've used this product for a few years to prevent my skin from ageing. It's perfect for dehydrated skin like mine. It consists of three types of hyaluronic acids, each of a different weight, that hydrate both on the surface and deep within the skin.

Step 4: Day Cream Line T by Susanne Kaufmann

This cream is based on active substances from botanical essences adapted for sensitive skin. It's anti-wrinkle and hydrating.

Step 5: Crème Contour des Yeux Biosensible eye cream by Biologique Recherche

The texture of this cream is perfect, as it's not too light or too greasy. It's a complete treatment to illuminate the eye area and prevent wrinkles.

Step 6: Ilia Skin Tint SFP 30 Super Serum

The last product I use borders on make-up rather than skincare, but I wanted to include it here as I haven't put on foundation since I discovered this serum. It gives an incredible glow and I really like the smell. It unifies the complexion and acts as a hydrating barrier on the skin. I recommend it for dry, dehydrated and sensitive skin, as well as normal skin.

Last note

By using effective and tailored skincare routines, I have really seen a difference in my skin's radiance and appearance. My skin is much smoother and more luminous than before. It is also worth noting that it's important to adapt your routine to the seasons, using products that are richer and more hydrating in winter, and lighter and slightly mattifying in summer. In summer, for example, I replace the Ilia Super Serum with Skin Perfect Primer 30 from Dermalogica. And don't forget to apply a cream with SPF at the end of your summer and winter routine!

A note on ageing

'At a certain age, you have to choose between your face and your ass'
Catherine Deneuve

As I stated in the introduction to this chapter, Parisiennes are less likely to go under the knife to preserve their youth, and I find that their attitude towards ageing is a lot healthier than that of many other countries and cultures. While in the US, for example, people might go to great lengths to try and preserve their youth, including having significant surgical procedures, you just don't see that type of work being done here. If Parisiennes do have work done, it's rarely visible – I think they are often genuinely proud of their wrinkles. Age here really does feel like it is just a number. At the start of their book *Older But Better, But Older*, Caroline de Maigret and Sophie Mas share a quote by Luis Buñuel: 'Age is something that doesn't matter, unless you are a cheese.' This phrase couldn't be more French, nor (in my opinion) could it ring more true. Since living in Paris, I've never felt the kind of social pressures around my age that I experienced when I lived in the UK. It feels like older women are more celebrated in France. Look at the likes of Juliette Binoche, Catherine Deneuve and fashion journalist Sophie Fontanel, for example – one of my favourite Instagram finds in the last couple of years. She wears her grey hair, age and wisdom with pride, and she's followed by young and old.

My tips for healthy & younger-looking skin

I will have turned thirty-eight years old by the time you read this book. Although, as I explained above, I don't feel the same sort of pressure around my age now that I live in Paris, I do often get asked about what I do to maintain healthy, younger-looking skin.  While great skincare products will aid you in your quest for youthful-looking skin, there are a few things that I've learned over the years, especially from my life in Paris, that I see as the foundations for healthy-looking skin. These aren't all products, though: they're behaviours and habits, too, that support healthy skin from within. So here are a few things that I try to practise regularly:

— Get enough sleep – I need around seven
  to eight hours of sleep a night.
— Drink plenty of water – around two litres a day.
  I always go to bed with a glass of water on my bedside
  table, so I can drink it if I get thirsty during the night.
  I also drink one or two big glasses of water soon after I
  wake up in the morning.
— Do high-intensity exercise – sweating helps purge your

skin of toxins, and will inadvertently make you drink more water.

— Avoid fatty and processed foods, as these will often dehydrate you and clog up your pores.

— Avoid sugar – it will not only cause your blood sugar levels to spike, meaning that you are likely to feel more tired after consuming it, but it can also cause acne.

— Avoid store-bought juices, as they're packed with sugar. The same goes for fizzy drinks.

— If you drink alcohol, drink good-quality and opt for red wine (which is high in antioxidants) over white, which mainly contains (you guessed it) sugar.

— Double cleanse. The first cleanse cleans your face of make-up, and the second cleans your skin and pores. You can use a cleansing oil or lotion to start, and then a lotion or gel to finish. I also love to use a detoxifying cleanser, such as the Purifying Cleanser by Tata Harper or the Eve Lom Cleanser, which you use with a hot cloth.

— Wear a serum morning and night under your moisturiser – I love Medik8 C-Tetra, Hyaluron Serum by Susanne Kaufmann, or Darphin Intral Serum for the morning; and Estée Lauder Advanced Night Repair or retinol serums by the likes of The Ordinary and Oskia at night.

— Wear a good eye cream morning and night – I like Eye Concentrate by La Mer, Eye Cream Line A by Susanne Kaufmann, Time Filler Eyes by Filorga and Caffeine Solution 5% by The Ordinary.

— Apply a moisturising cream with a minimum of SPF25 daily

— Use a flannel to help clean the make-up and cleanser off your face.

— Change your towels regularly, and have two towels – one for your body and smaller one for your face and hair.

— Avoid touching your face throughout the day.

— Wear tinted moisturiser rather than foundation.

— Eat fresh, seasonal foods.

— Get regular facials.

— Do a weekly mask – I love masks by Seed to Skin, Suzanne Kaufmann and Sisley.

— Practise regular face massage at home using a gua sha tool. I first discovered these around five years ago, thanks to the then-new Franco-Chinese brand Cha Ling L'Esprit du Thé. The design of these tools helps you to effectively massage the contours of your face, aiding circulation. This has an anti ageing effect and helps to boost the skin's plumpness.

— Don't over-exfoliate – but do exfoliate once a week to clean away dead cells.

— Sleep on silk pillows – they will help reduce wrinkles, as your skin will glide over them when you move in the night. And if you sleep with an eye mask, as I do, make sure it's made of silk and not too tight!

Plastic surgeon Dr Oren Marco's anti-ageing skincare routine tips

Dr Oren Marco (@docteurbeauty) is a plastic surgeon from Paris. He says: 'For me, there is no such thing as an ideal universal beauty routine: every routine can be good when it is adapted to the user, taking into account their skin, lifestyle, diet, age... So there isn't one particular miraculous brand that will work for everyone. A routine should include some simple principles, and once you find one that suits your skin, it shouldn't change too often.'

Tip 1: Cleansing

 The basis of everything is prevention. Gently cleanse your face twice daily, preferably with a cleansing oil, as it is gentler on the skin. The key is also to not over clean your face – if you do, the sebaceous glands can overreact by secreting too much sebum, which can cause imperfections.

Tip 2: Don't smoke

 When you smoke, the small vessels of the skin, called capillaries, become blocked; the skin is less well-vascularised, and therefore duller, dryer and less pink.

Tip 3: Moisturise

 After cleansing, morning and evening apply a protective moisturiser (one that suits your skin). And apply it using the 'face gym' technique, always lifting the skin of the face upwards.

Tip 4: Skin boosters

Finally, as a plastic surgeon, I recommend skin boosters (mesotherapy injections), where moisturising components are injected directly into the dermis (the deep layer of the skin), allowing a certain penetration of active compounds. This hydrates the skin and enhances its tone.

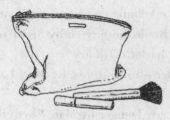

❧

My make-up bag essentials

— Tinted moisturiser – Laura Mercier Tinted Moisturizer
with SPF 30, Ilia Skin Tint SPF 30 Super Serum or
Les Beiges SPF 30 by Chanel
— Mascara – Le Volume de Chanel by Chanel, Le
Mascara by Rouje, So Stretch by Sisley or Push Up
Lashed by Charlotte Tilbury
— Eyelash curler – I own three, by Mac, Laura Mercier
and Rouje
— Lipstick – Lady Danger by Mac, Phyto Rouge no.40
by Sisley, Pillow Talk by Charlotte Tilbury and Rose
Pomette by Hermès
— Lip balm – Augustinus Bader or Hermès lip enhancer
— Nude lipliner – Pillow Talk by Charlotte Tilbury
— Cream eye shadow – Patine Bronze No. 840 by Chanel
— Concealer – by Laura Mercier or Giorgio Armani
— Bronzer – Filmstar Bronze & Glow by Charlotte Tilbury
— Translucent powder – by Laura Mercier or La Prairie
— Blush – Joues Contraste Malice No.71 by Chanel, Le
Phyto-Blush in Coral by Sisley and Multistick 'All of Me'
by Ilia
— Eyebrow pencil – by Sisley or Sensai
— Clear and coloured eyebrow gel – by Sisley
— Elizabeth Arden Eight Hour Cream
— Hand cream – by Aesop, Augustinus Bader, La Bastide
or Grown Alchemist

Juliette Levy's top tips for clean, healthy skin, and her morning skincare routine

Juliette (@juliettelevycohen) is the founder of Oh My Cream, a concept store dedicated to clean and luxury skincare and beauty products. They also carry their own affordable Oh My Cream skincare range, which they launched in 2017.

Tip 1: Double cleanse

It's the essential first step in a good skincare routine! First I apply Oh My Cream Skincare Cleansing Oil (which has a fresh citrus scent that I'm crazy about!). I apply it to my whole face, including on my eyes to remove mascara, then I rinse and follow with Cleansing Gel by Susanne Kaufmann, which leaves my skin fresh and clear without drying it out. Why double cleanse? To remove any dirt that has accumulated during the day (such as excess sebum, pollution and make-up), before deep cleaning your skin. If you don't double cleanse, it's a bit like taking a shower with your clothes on.

Tip 2: Exfoliate regularly

This is key to glowing and healthy skin! I am a fan of fruit acids, these small 'Pacman' molecules nibble and take off dead cells to reveal a fresh and luminous complexion. They are found in masks, lotions and exfoliating powders. For years, my favourite has been Dermalogica's Daily Microfoliant, but I also sometimes like to opt for a more concentrated version, such as the Liquid Mask from Oskia (which has a concentration of

10 per cent lactic acid!). I leave this on overnight and wake up with a baby-soft complexion.

Tip 3: Focus on hydration

Glowing skin is well-hydrated skin! For a long time, I made the mistake of trying to dry out imperfections. Instead, I now drink at least one and a half litres of water every day, and I use a lot of moisturiser (not too rich, of course, and without mineral oil or silicone if possible!). Mix your moisturiser with a good oil from time to time for a glowing finish. It's the secret to healthy, plump skin!

My morning skincare routine

I wake up and shower. I wash my body with Dr Bronner's invigorating Eucalyptus Liquid Soap and my hair (daily) with Rahua's Voluminous Shampoo – it's the best I've found for my fine, flat hair. After showering, I apply the Oh My Cream Skincare Universal Cream on my face – it provides maximum comfort without being greasy in a way that can block pores. Sometimes I take the time to massage it in with a gua sha tool. Two or three times a week, I exfoliate with Dermalogica's Daily Microfoliant, which helps fight a dull complexion and imperfections. Then I do a quick five-minute make-up routine: I even my complexion with PurePressed Base Mineral Foundation SPF20 by Jane Iredale, lift my cheekbones with a little blush, apply a good coat of Limitless Lash from Ilia and finish with a touch of Egyptian Magic on my lips. This is an all-purpose balm that's one of my essentials.

A chat about beauty, French skincare and body image with Emma Hoareau

'Skin influencer' and photographer Emma (@emmahoareau) was on my interview 'hit list' from the inception of this book. Although she's based in London, Emma spent her childhood in Paris (she is half French, half English) and, for me, she embodies the Parisian approach towards beauty and body image that I believe we can all learn from. She founded her blog, Lolita Says So, in 2009, while studying History of Art. At first, it was a place for her to share her photography, thoughts, travels and inspirations, but it quickly blossomed into somewhere she shared her favourite skincare and beauty tips as she began working in the industry. Today she shares her knowledge with an audience of more than 80,000 followers.

What inspired your interest in beauty and skincare?

I've always been a lover of beauty. And not just skincare – everywhere I look, I try to see the beauty. When I first graduated, I was offered a job as a beauty editor at a magazine and took it – even though my focus until then had been fashion – and within a month, I never wanted to work in anything else. Beauty is so interesting to me, as there's always something to learn and the technology and ingredients are constantly evolving. It fascinates me.

To me, you represent a very Parisian mentality when it comes to your approach to beauty, skincare and body image. What do you

think it is about the Parisian and French approach to skincare that sets it apart?

I grew up in Paris, and always loved the Parisian way of enjoying beauty products and going to the pharmacy, but not letting it become an obsession. To me, French beauty has a certain nonchalance to it – it's not that no one thinks about it, it's just that everyone accepts their own appearance more. No one is trying to look like another person – which, sadly, I think is now becoming more normalised elsewhere, with everyone wanting all the same features. I'm so glad I was brought up *a la Française* in this sense, as it's always made me enjoy my skin and body as they are. Of course, there are things we can work on, but it doesn't mean any part of oneself is 'wrong' or 'ugly' before.

You have been recognised by various publications now as being one of the UK's best beauty influencers – what is it you are doing differently, and how does that relate to your Parisian heritage?

Honestly it blows my mind this is the case, and I'm so thankful! I think it's because I share real skin and genuine, helpful information. I never use filters and know the importance of ingredients in skincare. I'm not here to pull the wool over anyone's eyes, but rather to share tips that can help your skin improve. And I think that's what people want and respond to: authenticity. I think what I learned from French culture when I was younger is that imperfection is perfection. Filtered skin doesn't look better to me, because I know it's not real. Pores are real, and realities are the most beautiful thing.

What are the aspects of French skincare that you love?

Using the same cream for your whole life! Of course, I test so many products for my job, but I love the notion of finding your core products and sticking to them because they work for you.

What is it about French pharmacy products do you think that has made them become so iconic?

They don't cost the earth – and they work! Such simplicity is key for skin. Not every product has to have a wonder ingredient. French pharmacy products use aspects of the French landscape – from grapes to *eau thermal* – to include as nourishing, calming and hydrating components of a product. It's also just so fun to find products that you can't get anywhere else but a French pharmacy. I always stock up when I'm in Paris!

What do you think we could and should be doing differently when it comes to beauty and skincare?

Enjoy it. Beauty is a ritual.

If you could choose only one product to use for the rest of your life, what would it be?

A hydrating serum.

If you could give one piece of advice for a skincare routine, what would it be?

Wear SPF!

Could you share a simple morning and evening routine?

Morning: cleanse, vitamin C serum, SPF.

Evening: double cleanse, salicylic acid toner, hydrating serum, cream.

What are you favourite French skincare brands?

Avène, La Roche-Posay, Bioderma, Vichy, Nuxe . . . all the classics I grew up using from the pharmacies in Paris.

What are you make-up bag essentials?

Brow gel and cream blush.

What do you do to relax?

Have a bath and make a giant cup of tea (there's the English side of me!).

What do you do to stay healthy and fit?

I do Pilates. I grew up training as a gymnast, and Reformer Pilates feels like a real workout. It keeps me flexible without being high impact.

Can you share some books that have inspired you?

A New Earth by Eckhart Tolle, *Ways of Seeing* by John Berger, *The Untethered Soul* by Michael A. Singer and *WomanCode* by Alisa Vitti.

What are your favourite places in Paris?

Le Bouillon Chartier for the vibe and old diner style – and the food, of course. Any café outdoors for watching the world go by, especially in Saint Germain, where I grew up. Le Bon Marché for wandering around and finding so many gems. It also reminds me of going there with my mother and sister when I was younger.

The hair affair

In April 2018, in the aftermath of a break-up, I cheated on my natural hair and dyed my hair blonde for the second time in my life. I had tried to do it a couple of years previously, when I went to a hair salon near Canal Saint Martin in the 10th arrondissement and declared, rather boldly, to the stylist that I wanted blonde hair. The stylist refused. Yes, you read that right: he said no to my request. I had never been told 'no' by a hair stylist before. Of course, they'd always advised me on my hair choices, but I'd never had one tell me that 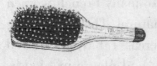 they would not carry out my request. But this is Paris. Oh, if only I had remembered that smart man's advice when I found someone else to bleach my hair a couple of years later as part of a paid collaboration with my Instagram account.

OK, so I loved my blonde hair for nearly two years. It breathed a little freshness into my appearance and attitude at a time when I was needing just that – a change in image, post break-up. I'd always heard that blondes have more fun – and I did have a lot of fun. But, slowly and surely, my hair began to break. My hair is very straight and very fine, and could not tolerate the bleach. In the autumn of 2019, after another relationship break-up, and with my hair looking like it was on its last legs, I decided enough was enough and went back to my natural colour.

It's funny how many friends have since commented on my hair, telling me how nice it looks and how much better it suits me this way. So, lesson learned: I should have listened to the first Parisian stylist I visited. At the time, as a compromise, that stylist gave me some natural-looking highlights that gave my hair a little sun-kissed glow. Ironically, that is exactly how I want my hair to look when it can hold a bit of colour again. Hopefully this tale will dissuade you from drastically changing your own hair colour in the future, and instead encourage you to cherish your natural locks. I'm telling you this story because I believe that the reason so many French women have such good hair is that it's natural. They rarely dye their hair different colours, whereas I have been red (verging on orange), plum, black and platinum blonde. But I'm finally taking heed of my fellow Parisiennes and letting my hair be as it should: natural.

❖

Hair products I swear by

— Shampoo – Voluminous Shampoo by Rahua and
7 Seconds Daily Shampoo by Unite

— I don't use a conditioner. Instead, I use hair cream
 – either Damage Remedy by Aveda or KMS Moist
 Repair Revival Creme
— When my hair is particularly dry, for example
 during summer, I apply oil to the ends – either
 Moroccanoil treatment by Moroccanoil or Precious
 Hair Care Oil by Sisley
— Scalp care – Scalp Scrub by Playa or Pramasana
 Purifying Scalp Cleanser by Aveda
— Hairdryer – Dyson
— Straighteners – GHD
— Dry shampoo – by Klorane or Playa
— Hairbrush – by Kent or the Radiance Brush by
 Sisley

Laurie Zanoletti's tips for healthy hair

Laurie (@lauriezanolettihair) is a Paris-based hair stylist and colourist. She has built up quite an Instagram following (134,000 at the time of writing) thanks to the long list of Parisian It-girls, models and publications she's worked with – not to mention her own rich brown luscious locks. She's an advocate for the 'just got out of bed' effortless look that the Parisiennes do so well, so I asked her for her top tips for healthy hair.

Use less product

The less you use, the better for the hair. I hate hairspray, for example. In fact, you can create a beautiful, natural look by simply working the hair with your fingers. This is better, as products will weigh down the hair, and they can make your hair become greasy or dried out faster. For me, the recipe for beautiful, shiny hair is shampoo and rinse. Better yet, shampoo your hair twice, use a good conditioner and then rinse well, so that when it comes to drying it, it's already shiny.

Eat a healthy diet

Our hair is a reflection of the food we eat, just like our skin, so it's super important to consume antioxidants, vegetables, fibre, protein, vitamins and fruit.

Cut your hair every two months

It's important to cut your hair by at least 1–2cm every two months if you don't want the ends to fray, and to keep your

hair beautiful and healthy. If there are a lot of split ends,
I suggest cutting 10 cm.

My favourite products

I love Mflorens Oil, which is 100 per cent vegan, completely
natural oil from Los Angeles. I use it on my roots twice a week.
I really like the products by Sébastien Pro, such as Thickefy
Foam Volumising Mousse for Fine Hair. I also like the Ultimate
Reset Mask Treatment by Shu Eumura, and I'm a fan of Color
Wow Dream Coat Supernatural Spray.

A note on hair removal and waxing

I had a whole debate with my current Parisian boyfriend about waxing at the start of our relationship, so I wanted to address the often contentious subject here. When we first started dating, he made a comment about my bikini line (or lack thereof). You see, I had been shaving or waxing off the entirety for years, as is very common in London. Interestingly, when I visited a well-known salon chain to get a wax when I first moved to Paris and asked for it all to be taken off, they wouldn't do it. I found this very surprising: the French usually have a very open and relaxed attitude towards nudity, so I wasn't expecting them to refuse. I wonder now if the aesthetician was subtly trying to let me know that it's 'not very Parisian' to get it all waxed off. According to a 2018 *Vogue* article, only one in three French women prefer to go hairless. Aurore Brahame, the aesthetician they interviewed, said: 'the trim, neat bush is definitely becoming more and more *au courant* [more common].'

These days, I go with the '*ticket metro*'. No, I'm not talking about the small white piece of cardboard that Parisians use to get around the city by public transport, I'm talking about a waxing style that one asks for when you visit a salon in Paris, which leaves you with something in the shape of a rectangular Metro ticket, not unlike the 'landing strip' you can ask for in British waxing salons.

What I've learned about body confidence, boobs and bras

'A girl comfortable in her skin is always sexy'
Yasmine Eslami

One very important lesson I've learned from my fellow Parisiennes, and one which ties in with their celebration of imperfection over perfection, as well as their ability to accept their flaws more easily, is to feel more confident about my body, flaws and all, and to accentuate what I do have. I have always been slim, and never worried too much about my weight or what I ate growing up, but one thing I always felt less secure about, throughout my teenage years and twenties, was the size of my bust. It's not that I was completely afraid of showing my breasts, I just didn't feel 100 per cent comfortable with it. From the moment I started wearing bras, I would do anything to make them look bigger, buying thick, padded styles from places like Etam to try to make me feel more 'womanly' and ultimately 'sexy'. Growing up with things like *Baywatch* and the other media that I was exposed to, I was left with an understanding of beauty that tied in with the 'Hollywood' look I mentioned earlier, and that meant bigger breasts were more beautiful, and a heaving cleavage was the epitome of sexiness – and of being a woman. So I tried to enhance my smaller chest to conform to this concept of feminine beauty. A trip to buy a new bra was always an agonising and often embarrassing experience, as the styles I really wanted to wear, namely underwired, padded and push-up – think Victoria's Secret, because that was the trend at the time – never fitted me properly. I don't remember there being a lot of choice in smaller sizes. I was also influenced by the fact that my mother had a breast enlargement in her forties, when I was fourteen, just as her own mother had done in California in the sixties: they, too, thought bigger was more feminine and beautiful.

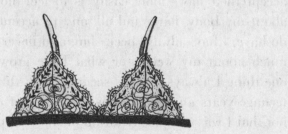

Since living in Paris, however, I have come to accept and be rather proud of what I have, as here, I've never been made to feel that the smaller size of my bust makes me less beautiful, sexy or feminine. Of course, it helps that, historically, the Parisian woman has been personified by the likes of Jane Birkin, her daughters and Vanessa Paradis, famous icons who are more petit and generally have less going on in the boob department.

Perhaps I had just moved to a city where my smaller chest was more in vogue. It's a sentiment that Monica de La Villardière echoed when I interviewed her (see page 82 for her full interview): 'Being flat-chested is also considered attractive here – it's deemed sexy if you have a small chest and wear a tank top for example that skims your nipples. That is a huge look in Paris, because you're playing up your attributes, whatever they may be.'

But I also believe that here, there is less of a focus on any one size being 'better' than another. The women around me, my friends and the press all find sexiness and femininity in an attitude or character, rather than a prescribed set of physical attributes. It's an important point about the Parisian view of beauty, and, as such, a good lesson to learn: play up your attributes, rather than focusing on your flaws. I find the way that Parisian women conduct and present themselves so empowering. I have since ditched the padding and now opt only for dainty mesh or lace bras, which are much chicer and highlight my figure in other ways.

I mentioned plastic surgery above, and it's worth noting that the French attitude that big is not necessarily better also extends to plastic surgery. Although some French women do indeed opt for breast augmentation, they tend not to go for overly large sizes, and there's an emphasis on maintaining a look that's very natural, so that one cannot easily tell if they've had work. A 2017 *Times* article also describes a new kind of aesthetic that is 'decidedly French' and a 'backlash against the overblown, over-pumped, overfilled, over-frozen surgery that has had the celebrity world – scratch that, the entire Western world – in its grip for the past ten or so years . . . We've been routinely, relentlessly exposed to "work" – whether it be on the red carpet, on reality television or even on the school run.'

It's an outlook that is reinforced by my friend Dr Oren Marco (who gave me his anti-ageing skincare tips on page 118), who recently posted: 'Do not confuse improving with transforming. Improve or erase a complex, yes, but to modify one's features for no real reason, just to follow an aesthetic fashion trend: NO!'

Ultimately, the moral of the story is that body confidence comes from within, not from what you look like, nor from following trends in the beauty industry. Enjoy what you've got, and have fun making the most of it. And if you do want to change something about yourself, don't do it because you are following a trend or subscribing to a notion of beauty that is completely different to your own.

A note on nudity

I think the French celebration and appreciation of all different body types partly comes from the fact that, in France, nudity is regarded as less of a taboo. Showing more flesh doesn't immediately equate to being more sexual; publications show the nipple, and it's also legal to sunbathe topless on beaches. (The only reason that French women might bare less skin on the beach these

days is the prevalence of social media and not wanting
half naked photos of themselves ending up on someone
else's Instagram feed.)

You only have to look at some of the most popular
French influencers on Instagram, such as Anne-Laure
Mais, Sabina Socol, Emma Hoareau, and model and
influencer Clara Barry to see that French women are not
afraid to show more skin. I believe this is because they
grew up in a society that was more comfortable with the
idea. Last year, a *New York Times* article noted that: 'In
France, where the bikini was invented nearly seventy-five
years ago, being topless has been associated with women's
liberation since various movies in the 1960s and 1970s
showed actresses like Brigitte Bardot or Miou-Miou bare-
breasted outside.' Emma Hoareau, who I spoke to earlier
in this section (see page 123), told me: 'It's funny to me
that the norm is that someone would be afraid to show
their skin or their body. It's like it's programmed into
us that something about our body or flesh especially
as women – is shameful. To me all skins and bodies are
beautiful, and showing your body isn't shameful, showing
off, nor sexual. It's your physical shell! I definitely think
there is something French about not seeing body parts
as sexual or shameful. If you've ever been to a beach in
France, you'll know the ease with which people sunbathe
topless or nude – it is the total norm.'

Tips to help you boost your body confidence
the *au naturel* way

— Wear attractive and comfortable underwear. If in doubt, go for something lacy and black. Don't wear padded bras if you have small boobs – this will often make them look smaller, as the bra can gape at the top. Besides, as it says in *The Times* article I cited earlier, the 'push-up look is passé'. And, of course, always make sure you're wearing the right size bra!

— Wear high-waisted, bum-hugging jeans or skirts and dresses that accentuate your waist.

— I've talked above about how nudity and showing some skin doesn't have to be sexualised, but in the same way, if you would like to feel a bit sexy, it's often better to leave a little to the imagination. In France, a woman might sunbathe topless just to enjoy the feeling of the sun on her skin and to have a more even tan, but if she wants to looks sexy, she might wear a figure-skimming tank top, as Monica described above, rather than trying to show too much cleavage.

— Do not continuously point out your flaws to friends and lovers.

— Walk around naked in front of your lover; they will find it sexy, and it will make you feel more confident.

— Walk with your head held high and shoulders back.

— Take ballet classes to help with posture.

— Move in the morning – stretch, do yoga or take a cardio class. (Exercise can help you connect with your body and promote the release of 'happy hormones' to help ward off depression and will ultimately make you feel more confident.)

— Do not eat carbs in the morning, as they can leave you feeling bloated. Avoid them last thing at night, too – your metabolism will have a harder time digesting them while you sleep.
— Again, don't consume too much sugar.
— Go easy on the alcohol – a hangover will do nothing for your confidence. In fact, alcohol is a depressant. Plus it can be packed full of calories, and often makes you feel bloated.
— Don't wear too much foundation, as it clogs pores.
— Do wear a red lip.

❧

My favourite French lingerie brands to make you feel body confident and beautiful

Many of the Parisian clothing brands I wrote about in the Fashion & Style chapter also offer lingerie, for example Sézane and Rouje, but there are a few Parisian brands that specialise in beautiful lingerie to help you make the most of your body and feel comfortable in your own skin. Here are my favourites:

ERES – Former ERES designer Valérie Delafosse once said: 'I don't follow trends; I don't even know what they are. I just follow my own intuition.' ERES has a very Parisian focus on the timeless quality of design over fashion fads, which has made it one of the most renowned swimwear and lingerie brands in the world. Another reason for the brand's popularity is the fact that their shapes have been specifically designed to mould to the female body and will flatter most figures. Founded in 1968 by Irène Leroux, ERES is synonymous with Parisian style and their now iconic black one-piece was described by British fashion editor Hilary Alexander as 'the Coco Chanel of swimsuits'.

Yasmine Eslami – Yasmine Eslami created her eponymous line of lingerie in 2011, and in 2015 the launch of her swimwear offering coincided with her appointment as Artistic Director of swimwear and beachwear for ERES, where she designed the collections for summers 2016 and 2017. While her lingerie is, of course, designed to seduce (it's Parisian, after all), what matters most to Eslami is the way the pieces *make the wearer feel*. As she pointed out in an interview with *Marie Claire*, 'Many brands focus their discourse on seduction, with reference to men. However, if my cuts are sensual, I believe that a woman has her own identity and that she pleases herself.'

YSÉ – Since 2012, YSÉ, founded by Clara Blocman, has been producing beautifully flattering lingerie, created by women for women. The shapes and the materials they use enhance the silhouette, and they promote all types of bodies, regardless of size, skin colour and age. I particularly love the fact that they do not digitally retouch their models' skin, so that you can see the 'imperfections' – lines, cellulite and wrinkles – which, you know by now, are the things that make our bodies beautiful and unique.

Julie Pujols Benoit's three exercises for a perky derrière

Julie (@juliepujols) is a wellbeing journalist, Pilates instructor and creator of the 'Méthode Pilates Booty'.

She says that one needs to do *'polyarticulaire'* movements (using various muscles and joints at the same time) and work the legs. Here's her mini 15-minute training, based on three different exercises. She advises completing this three times a week.

Exercise 1

Squats are the most efficient exercise for shaping a nice bum. Do 25 squats, followed by 10 small bouncing movements, then pause and then start again. Repeat for four sets. It will only take two to three minutes.

Exercise 2

Next, lie on your back with your arms by your sides, tummy pulled in, legs bent and feet against your bum. As you breathe out, lift your hips towards the sky and contract your bum muscles. As you breathe in, lower your bottom, but don't touch the floor. Repeat this 50 times.

Exercise 3

Lie on your side and bend your knees so they are level with your belly button, then lift your top knee towards the sky. Do this 50 times on each side. To make it harder, you can loop a resistance band around your knees.

Julie's tips for keeping her figure

In the morning I drink a big glass of matcha tea before eating anything. I eat healthily, but I don't put too much pressure on myself. I also eat lots of protein to maintain my muscles. And when I'm in the car or on public transport, I do subtle glute exercises, like squeezing my buttocks.

I do dry body brushing every morning, starting with my feet and brushing up towards my head. I use a brush from Aime skincare. I then apply Caudalie Lift & Firm Body Cream Vinosculpt.

My best tip for reducing and avoiding cellulite is to accompany the application of body cream with a self-massage, palpitating your skin as you work the cream into it. I also visit Martine de Richeville, whose manual remodelling technique is the best at targeting cellulite.

A note on wellbeing

'I think we Parisians can be full of contradictions:
we want to be healthy, yet we have long dinners and
get up late, so we don't have time to work out;
we basically like to show the world what
good hedonists we can be!'
Caroline Perrineau

In most areas of their lives, as I've already explained, the Parisiennes practise a more laidback approach; they err on the side of caution when it comes to new trends (rarely following them) and don't easily get sucked into the latest fads. Paris sometimes has a reputation for being less innovative and less open to change. This can be frustrating to some, but it can also be seen as advantageous, as they don't rush to change. Instead, they adopt new ideas slowly, which I think is a healthier way. This is certainly true for the wellbeing industry in Paris. When it comes to wellness, they do what they need to do for their body and mind, without getting obsessed or going overboard. Personally, I practise yoga when I need to, and the same goes for meditation. I would love to say that it is part of my daily routine – and perhaps one day it will be – but I also don't think it's healthy to get obsessed with it, as that would contradict why I'm doing it in the first place.

The Parisian approach is more 'organic', as yoga practitioner and teacher Caroline Perrineau (@theyoginist)
told me when I asked her about how she approaches
wellbeing and adopting a healthier lifestyle. I went on a
press trip to Marrakesh with Caroline a couple of years
ago, and found her teaching method very relaxed and, as
such, reassuring and refreshing. She advises her students
to do as much they can and at their own pace, whereas
I've had yoga teachers physically force me into positions
in the past. Caroline told me: 'I do believe health starts
from within, it has to have a meaning to you, a feeling
of rightness, especially as there is no "one-size-fits-all"
solution in that domain.'

Caroline's decision to become a yoga teacher five
years ago came just at the right time, as the practice
was gaining popularity. But I think it's her relaxed and
positive attitude that has also helped drive her following
(135,000 at the time of writing). 'Paris has been my
hometown for long enough that I got to experience for
myself its advantages and drawbacks, which are the ones
found in many big cities: stress, anxiety, pollution, loss of
purpose, etc.,' she says. '[I realised] I needed to change
my lifestyle by including yoga in it, and naturally came
to the conclusion I could also maybe spread this "goodness" around, and start teaching yoga.' And her captions
(in English) do indeed spread goodness: they are neither
preachy nor pushy.

The wellbeing industry is finally gathering some speed
in Paris, with the launch of wellbeing-focused skincare

brands like Aime and Holidermie, new gym spaces like Dynamo Cycling, Montgolfière, Episod and Tiger Yoga Studio, and classes such as Sophie Trem's Good Mood Class and Lili Barbery's Kundalini yoga class, but it's still quite new and niche, as Caroline goes on to explain: 'The wellbeing industry isn't so well developed, compared to the US or England, yet it is expanding little by little.'

Caroline Perrineau's top tips for finding calm in a city

Focus on:

— breathing

— movement

— meditation (in all its many forms)

For me, these are three great tools to use when in need.

To calm myself, I like to take ten to fifteen slow, deep breathes, inhaling and exhaling for a count of four to start with, which I may then increase.

When I am in need of more guidance, I like to listen to short meditation sessions on various apps (I like the app Insight Timer, which has some great ones – and for free).

Melanie Huynh's 'inside out' morning and evening skincare routine

Melanie (@melaniehuynh1) is a former stylist who began her career at *French Vogue* as assistant to the then editor-in-chief Carine Roitfeld. While on the magazine, she spent some time working on the beauty pages with beauty editor Frederique Verley, and developed a passion for skincare, beauty and wellbeing. In 2019, she launched Holidermie, a French skincare and wellbeing brand that focuses on 'inside out' beauty. She is at the forefront of wellbeing within skincare in Paris, so I wanted to ask her for her morning and evening skincare routine.

Morning routine

I usually wake up before my children, at around 6.30–6.45 a.m. I go to my bathroom and the first thing I do is clean my tongue and do oil pulling with coconut oil. I've been doing this for many years now: I use a tongue cleaner from Cosmic Dealer, founded by Monique Foy. I splash cold water on my face, then light a candle and do 5 minutes of meditation on my Holidermie mat (I also use a Tibetan bowl). I drink some warm water to detox, then I do some dry brushing and jump in the shower. I wash my hair with Holidermie, Cut by Fred or Leonor Greyl shampoo. I always try to finish with a burst of cold water to wake me up.

After my shower, I apply my Holi Body lotion. Then I use Holidermie Initiation Essentielle lotion to balance the pH of my skin, before applying Nutrition Sublime oil with my cold gua sha. I do some face yoga (I follow the techniques shared by our Holidermie experts, such as Sylvie Lefranc, and I also like Aurélia del Sol and @faceyogamethod). Next I apply Régénération Concentrée serum and Protection Urbaine day cream. Then, I put on some make-up. I like to use my friend's brand, VIOLETTE_FR (which launched in early 2021) or Hermès. I also love the lipsticks from La Bouche Rouge. I like curling my eyelashes, and I use either Chanel or Dior mascara. After this, I wake up my children (I have two girls, aged seven and twelve), then head into the kitchen. I take a Holidermie food supplement, HoliMoist, with a glass of beauty powder with adaptogens. Then I make a cup of Holidermie Elixir de Beauté. Once I've taken my children to school, I try to do an hour of exercise, either Ashtanga yoga, boxing or running. I always leave the house with a bottle filled with Holi Glow Drops.

Evening routine

I use Holidermie products, of course! I remove my make-up with Emulsion Démaquillante and apply serum, followed by Régénération Fondamentale evening cream. Then I might do some more face yoga or Korean lift, which is good for lymphatic drainage. I like to make a nighttime infusion with the Holidermie beauty powder 'Poudre de Sommeil', and I use an Aveda Chakra spray on my silk pillow. I put on some Holidermie hand cream and lip baume. I like to read before sleeping – and I always turn off my phone.

Other products I love are the bath salts from Costa Brazil, palo santo and sage from Sentara and Etoile Nomade, body

scrub and foot cream by Suzanne Kaufmann, adaptogens from
Anima Mundi Herbals, and perfumes by Dorsay and Byredo.

My favourite wellbeing-focused places in Paris

Eateries: Wild & the Moon, Maisie and Guinguette d'Angèle,
Sol Semilla, 42 Degrés.

Yoga: Kshanti, Tigre Yoga, Bloom for meditation, Reformation.

Skincare and wellbeing: Holidermie Loft for face treatment
and GMP red light dome; Seemycosmetics for HydraFacial;
Elaine Huntzinger for acupuncture and facials; Barbara
Sand for Kobido. I also love face massages with Sylvie
Lefranc.

Healthy tips to live by from Sofiia Manousha

Sofiia (@sofiiamanousha) is an actress and director, and the founder of My Beautyfuel Food (mybeautyfuelfood.com), a site dedicated to wellness, the impact our diet has on the skin, and how to feel good about yourself, inside and out. She has a holistic view of beauty and wellbeing, which, although changing, is still rather rare in Paris. She began practising yoga fifteen years ago, which made her feel like an 'alien' as no one else was doing it at the time. To her, wellbeing is a state of mind: 'Everything is linked: our food and our lifestyle are our cellular fuel; one does not go without the other. I place a lot of importance on my sleep, and I hydrate myself (I drink a lot of water and vegetable juices, which are extraordinary for mineralising the body).' Here's what she does to maintain a healthy and balanced lifestyle.

What do you do to relax?
I switch off my phone, light a candle and burn some palo santo. I also like to draw while listening to classical music, or I'll take a bath. When I'm on set filming, I often live in hotels, so I always ask for a room with a bathtub – I just add bath salts and relax. From Friday evening to Monday morning, I take a break from social media. As soon as I can, I will walk in the forest, or I will return to the Atlas Mountains in Morocco to recharge my batteries.

What is your morning routine?
I usually wake up quite early. I then go to the bathroom to use

my tongue scraper (not very glamorous, but it's very effective in eliminating the toxins accumulated during the night), then I do a dry brushing (to stimulate the lymph and promote blood circulation). After this, I take a cold shower – it may sound extreme, but it's amazing for the immune system and blood circulation, and I feel so good afterwards. I drink about 1 litre of water while doing my facial gym (I'm a big fan of gua sha). I then make my morning elixir of apple cider vinegar, ten drops of lemon and lukewarm water, which helps to alkalise the body and boost digestion. I follow that up with a stomach vacuum, which helps to purify the organs through ventral breathing (my sister, Anais Jazmine, created a 'Belly Sculpting' technique), followed by a twenty-five-minute yoga/Pilates flow, and finally five minutes of meditation.

What do you do to stay fit and healthy?

My morning routine is essential for my wellbeing: I need this time for myself. I usually make myself an adaptogen drink using cocoa, reishi, chaga mushrooms and raw manuka honey. Adaptogens are magic for the nervous system and health. I really like vegetable juices. I try to get enough sleep, and I love to recharge my batteries in the mountains or go surfing as soon as I return to Morocco. I do a lot of sport: boxing, swimming, Reformer, Gyrotonic and Pilates with my coach Verena Tremel at Studio Rituel and Megaformer with Marcia Segal at Snake & Twist. I cannot imagine my life without sport. I also laugh a lot.

What is your skincare routine?

In the morning, I do a facial gym (as explained above), then I apply Active Treatment Essence from Vintner's Daughter, followed by a serum by Darphin (excellent for the radiance of the complexion), and finally my moisturiser, which I've been using for a while, 'The Cream' by Augustinus Bader. In the evening, I practise double cleansing. I use On the Wild Side cleansing oil, made by an organic French brand using wild plants, and then a Susanne Kaufmann cleanser. I follow this with an Aurélia skincare serum with CBD, and lastly Odacité night cream. I prefer clean products. Once a month I treat myself to a kobido facial or hydrafacial at SeeMy Cosmetics, and I regularly go to Mélanie Calzada, my facialist, for a body remodelling and a face miracle.

What are your favourite beauty tips?

I regularly make homemade face masks. I mix together honey, coconut sugar, matcha and rose water, apply it and leave it on for thirty minutes. And I often rinse my hair with apple cider vinegar, which makes it shiny.

What are your favourite places in Paris?

Studio Rituel for Reformer Pilates, yoga and Gyrotonics; the Hoy Hotel for lunch; Passager Café for coffee; and Maison Suissen for their belly massage followed by green tea to relax. I really like to hunt through Les Puces (the flea markets) in Saint Ouen for vintage dishes at the stand La Tablée d'Elo, and the Picasso Museum always has beautiful exhibitions. I visit O'kari Hammam for a moment of relaxation and change of scenery: it's one of my favourite places to recharge my batteries

❖

Sofiia's 'Baby Face' smoothie recipe

Ingredients

100g beetroot

½ ripe banana

juice of ½ lemon

handful of baby spinach leaves

handful of frozen mango

1 teaspoon baobab powder

1 teaspoon klamath powder

1 tablespoon hemp protein

2cm piece of fresh turmeric

2cm piece of fresh ginger

½ teaspoon rose water

1 teaspoon almond butter

235ml coconut water (or almond milk for an even
    creamier texture)

Method

Place all the ingredients in a high-powered blender
(I use a Vitamix) and blend until you obtain a liquid
and creamy texture. Pour into a tall glass. If you like,
you can scatter some seeds, raw cocoa or pollen on top –
whatever makes you happy and will do your body good.

Perfume and scent

'You should put scent where you like to be kissed'
Catherine Deneuve

Finding the scent that is right for you is important to many Parisians – so much so that even the Parisian men I've met have a favourite fragrance that they've worn for years and are proud of it. As with fashion and skincare, it's no surprise to learn that Paris has a long history with the creation of perfume. As I mentioned earlier, France is home to Grasse, which has been the world's most famous perfume-making region since the fourteenth century, and is where Paris' most iconic perfumes are still made today. Along with Italy, France emerged as the fragrance capital of Europe in the 1500s. During the reign of Louis XIV, perfume was often substituted for soap and water, and by the eighteenth century, Grasse was the epicentre for European perfume creations. Parisian perfume was even immortalised by German writer Patrick Suskind in his bestselling book, *Perfume: The Story of a Murderer*. Thanks to my job, I've been lucky enough to try a whole library's worth of perfumes, but there are a few that I personally love, and that make me feel a little more feminine and elegant when wearing them.

Five French fragrances, old and new, that will make you feel a little more Parisian

L'Eau d'Hadrien by Goutal – Founder Annick Goutal's first love was the piano, and as a child she dreamed of becoming a pianist, until her looks matched her creative talent and she began modelling. But it was a meeting with a perfumer from Grasse that finally cemented her *raison d'être*. Inspired, she began making her own fragrances in 1979. In 1981, she established her eponymous perfume house, and with it, launched what is today one of Paris's most iconic scents: L'Eau d'Hadrien. The fragrance was inspired by the novel *Memoirs of Hadrian* by Marguerite Yourcenar, detailing Roman Emperor Hadrian's death, and it is a celebration of all things Tuscan, from its sunshine to the terraces lined with Cypress trees, with notes of Sicilian lemon. It put Goutal on the fragrance map and firmly established the brand within the perfume industry. It was also the scent the *maison* gifted to Princess Diana on the birth of Harry, for any royal fans reading this book!

L'Eau Diptyque – When writing about Diptyque, I discovered that the brand is named after the art term 'diptych' (spelled *'diptyque'* in French) – meaning an artwork with two panels, often attached by a hinge. To the three founders (a painter, an interior architect and a theatre set designer) this name perfectly embodied their interests, and the space they'd found for their new boutique on 32 Boulevard Saint-Germain, which had two identical windows flanking the front door. Here, they were planning on selling an array of elegant found goods, lifestyle wares and their own colourful fabrics. When they opened their doors in 1961, their bazaar (or 'concept store' in today's terms) became an instant hit. In 1963, they began making candles inspired by their fabric colours, and the candle maker suggested they add scents to them, helping to create the brand we know today. They celebrated their third year of business with three candles scented with hawthorn, cinnamon and tea. In 1964, the *maison* dipped its toe into the world of beauty, when it began importing perfumes by the British perfume house Penhaligon's, followed by violet oatmeal facemasks by Rimmel. This foray into the cosmetic industry sparked a keen interest in beauty products, and the founders began conjuring up ideas for perfumes and creams, which the house is now just as famous for. For me, Diptyque embodies the essence of Paris – artistic, hedonistic, playful, seductive, curious, elegant and a little bit strange. And while it has been commercialised to great success, it is still one of my go-to brands for unique presents.

My favourite Diptyque scent is L'Eau, which was, incidentally, their very first fragrance, created in 1968. It's a little spicy, with notes of cinnamon, clove, geranium and wood, but none of them are overpowering, and the perfume can be worn by both men and women.

Chanel No.5 Eau de Parfum – An obvious choice, perhaps, but I cannot talk about French fragrances without mentioning the city's most iconic scent, Chanel No. 5. This perfume is just as popular today as it was when it was created in 1921 by the fashion house as their first foray into fragrance. It's also made in exactly the same way as it was nearly one hundred years ago, as I discovered at an exhibition last autumn in Paris's Muséum national d'Historie naturelle (Natural History Museum), which was celebrating Chanel's rich history with botanicals. The formula for Chanel No. 5 was crafted by French-Russian perfumer Ernest Beaux using ylang-ylang, may rose and jasmine, and was originally created to celebrate the 'liberated feminine spirit of the 1920s'.

The story behind the name is just as interesting. Between the ages of twelve and eighteen, Gabrielle Chanel spent her youth in a strict convent, which is where her associations with the number five began. To her, it signified purity and her daily pilgrimage to the Cathedral to pray, following paths that were laid out in circular patterns repeating the number five. When presented with the choice of numbered perfume vials created by Beaux, she unsurprisingly chose number 'five' – she was also already showing her collections on the fifth of May – the fifth month of the year, which she believed brought her good luck.

Tonka 25 by Le Labo – Le Labo is actually a New York-born brand, but its co-founder Fabrice Penot is from Paris. The fragrances are also made in Grasse, so that makes it Parisian enough for me. Tonka 25 has swiftly become one of my favourite scents. It took three years to conceive – they say the best things come to those who wait, and that is certainly true of this scent. I'm very fussy when it comes to fragrance, as I have a very strong sense of smell and there are quite a few famous perfumes that give me headaches, but when I first caught a whiff of Tonka 25 at a Le Labo boutique in London, I was immediately enamoured with it and wore it every day until the bottle ran out.

Santal Massoia by Hermès – This is a personal favourite, and I almost don't want to give the name away, but I'm here to give you tips on how to be a little more Parisian, so I will. This particular fragrance – not one of their most famous, but by far my favourite from the Hermès fragrance range – is part of the Hermessence collection, which celebrates nature and raw materials, and, according to creator Jean-Claud Ellena, symobolises 'creative freedom and a highly individual writing style'. It perfectly blends cedar, sandalwood and massoia – a tropical tree native to New Guinea, whose bark has a sweet aroma. This combination creates a warming scent that hits just the right note on the sweet spectrum, so that it is seductive, but subtle and not overpowering. The Hermès fragrance story began in 1951 with Eau d'Hermès, which was created by one of the greatest talents in the world of perfumery at the time, Edmond Roudnitska. Ten years later came Caleche, the maison's first women's perfume, composed by Guy Robert. This launch established

Hermès as a major player and a coveted luxury brand in the perfume industry. Their scents are pricey, but worth the investment, as they are unique enough that you will stand out when wearing one, but subtle enough not to be detected.

Ambre Chic by Nout – New to the fragrance market as of 2020, Nout is an organic and vegan fragrance brand that has also been Cosmos Organic certified (an international standard for organic and natural cosmetic products that was implemented in 2010). The brand uses only natural ingredients free from synthetic fragrances, without the dyes or petrochemicals that can often be found in other fragrances. The scents are also created in Grasse, and Ambre Chic is my pick as it has some of my favourite fragrance notes, such as bergamot, vanilla and cedar.

⚜

Tips for wearing and caring for your perfume

— Use no more than four spritzes – one on each wrist, and one on either side of your neck, just under your jaw line. Or a spritz behind each ear is also good.
— Don't *rub* your wrists together – the heat of rubbing them together can change the chemistry of the perfume.

— Don't spritz perfume on your clothes if you can
help it: the ingredients can damage clothing.
— Do not keep your perfume bottles near a radiator
nor in a steamy bathroom.

❖

ADDRESS BOOK

Beauty and skincare

Biologique Recherche *(www.biologique-recherche.com
– 32 Avenue des Champs-Elysées, 75008)*

Darphin Institute *(www.darphin.fr –
350 rue Saint-Honoré, 75001)*

Le Bon Marché *(24 Rue de Sèvres, 75007)*

L'Officine Universelle Buly *(www.buly1803.com –
6 Rue Bonaparte, 75006)*

Maison Sisley *(www.sisley-paris.com.com –
5 Avenue de Friedland, 75008)*

Oh My Cream (also offer facials) *(www.ohmycream.
com – multiple locations)*

Sophie Carbonari *(www.sophiecarbonari.com)*

Fragrance

Annick Goutal *(www.goutalparis.com – multiple
locations)*

Diptyque *(www.diptyque.com – multiple locations)*

Ex Nihilo *(www.ex-nihilo-paris.com –
352 Rue Saint-Honoré, 75001)*

L'Artisan Parfumeur *(www.artisanparfumeur.com –
209 Rue Saint-Honoré, 75001)*

Nose *(www.noseparis.com – 20 Rue Bachaumont,
75002)*

Trudon *(www.trudon.com – 11 Rue Sainte-Croix,
75004)*

Body massage

Martine de Richeville *(www.martinedericheville.com –*
13 Boulevard Malesherbes, 75008)

Nails

Kure Bazaar *(www.kurebazaar.com –*
Le Bon Marché, 24 Rue de Sèvres, 75007)
The Manucurist *(www.manucurist.com –*
19 Rue d'Enghien, 75010)

Hair

Christophe Robin *(www.christopherobin.fr –*
16 Rue Bachaumont, 75002)
David Mallett *(david-mallett.com –*
14 Rue Notre Dame des Victoires, 75002)

Interiors & home life

Parisians at home

'One art in particular is very Parisian: the art of
expressing your taste through the way you dress
or in the way you decorate your apartment'
Jeanne Damas and Lauren Bastide, *In Paris*

Much like their approach to fashion, Parisians don't
tend to follow trends in the home. They mix old with
new, and their homes reflect their personalities and lives
rather than any one style. However seemingly ideal their
lives might look, things are never actually perfect, and
decoration often occurs in a more laid-back, random
and wholly personal way. There might be a piece of
mid-century furniture, such as a console table, some
books stacked in a corner with a potted plant placed on
top, framed taxidermy butterflies on the
wall, a record player, vintage artworks
and colourful throws and cushions. As
such, since I moved to Paris, I've been
less strict about sticking to any one dom-
inant style, and, often influenced by
Parisian buildings themselves,
have become less afraid when
it comes to mixing modern with
vintage. In her book, *Maison:*

Parisian Chic at Home, which she co-wrote with illustrator and boutique-owner Marin Montagut, Inès de La Fressange says: 'Their guiding principle is to combine everything: the new with the old, the sophisticated with the antiquated, the luxurious with the simple. Furniture can be stripped, distressed or restored – as long as the result exudes charm.' This, for me, helps to sum up a Parisian's sense of interior style. Although they do not follow any one trend, there are some common threads – they love vintage, unique objects, and enjoy mixing old with new. And (again, as when selecting clothing) comfort is a key word: they want their spaces to be not only beautiful to look at, but also comfortable to live in.

With their reputation for favouring a more minimal range of hues when it comes to fashion, a Parisian interior can be more eclectic and colourful than you might expect. A good example of this are the designs by renowned interior designer Dorothée Meilichzon (who designed the interiors of Hotel des Grand Boulevards, the restaurant Balagan and the interiors for the Experimental Group), and the home of Sarah Poniatowski, founder of Maison Sarah Lavoine (she gives me her tips for using colour at home on page 168). In many ways, Parisian interior style is difficult to define, but I have found there are a few running themes, including personal objects, inherited items, photos, treasures brought back from travels, vintage pieces bought at *brocantes* (vintage markets) or on Selency (I will chat to the site's co-founder, Charlotte Cadé, on page 235). Another key theme is making the most of what they have, because the old buildings we live in here in Paris can be unforgiving at times, and the spaces can also be tiny! There's a seeming effortlessness in the Parisian approach to interior decorating: spaces often take on a life of their own, with collections of knick-knacks cobbled together and displayed in a nonchalant way that naturally ends up looking aesthetically pleasing, and above all lived-in and cosy! As Lauren Bastide, journalist, podcaster and co-author of *In Paris*, says: 'We believe it's essential to make our homes incredibly comfortable, whether we have an opulent apartment or a small attic room. We add candles, cushions, old books and soft sofas to create a place for working, dreaming, procrastinating and entertaining friends on Friday and Saturday evenings, because it's so much better when everyone comes to us.'

A space for entertaining friends in is very high on a Parisian's interior priority list. Despite their love of travel, café culture and dining out, Parisians are homebodies at heart, and although they might not cook big, extravagant meals, they do love to gather at home. So, regardless of the size of the space they inhabit, they create havens in their homes, cosy spaces where they can socialise with friends. *Apéros* turn into dinner and suddenly become parties as more friends arrive. I've spent numerous nights at my friend Magali's (who I speak to in the Relationships, Love & Dating chapter), for example, with a multitude of friends, new friends, old friends, with more and more people arriving until, by the end of the evening,

it is indeed a party. Times spent at Magali's are exactly
as Bastide describes in *In Paris*: 'Parisians have the most
fun when they're at a friend's place, dancing around a
turntable or speaker, taking breaks from time to time
to smoke cigarettes and philosophise, eight squeezed
on to the balcony.' And so their spaces take on the shape
of a home, sleeping space, dance floor and restaurant, all
rolled into one. And even when they have small children,
this doesn't stop them – I've been to various *apéros* or
dinners where the children of guests will either bunk with
the host's children or doze off on the adults' bed while we
wile away the night drinking and dancing in the *salon*.

Art and design also play a vital role in a Parisian's
life – after all, it is, arguably, the most beautiful city in
the world. I have come to believe that living in a city like
Paris, so steeped in culture, literature and art, and filled
to the brim with beautiful historical buildings, picturesque squares and stunning views, coupled with a wealth
of art galleries and museums, has heightened Parisians'
awareness of aesthetics and finessed their tastes. Their
spaces thoughtfully and artfully reflect their personalities
and interests, and, as a result, I find their interior style
warm, cosy, surprising, quirky, approachable and, most
of, all beautiful. Parisians are natural stylists, curating
home environments in a way that seems so effortless,
yet put-together and stylish, such as the eclectic space
of Eugénie Trochu, digital fashion editor for *Vogue Paris*,
who tells me about a few of her favourite pieces at home
on page 225. But you don't have to live in Paris to harness

these aesthetics and inject a more Parisian way of styling into your home.

And that's what I am going to talk about in this section. I will also share my own experiences of flat-hunting (no easy feat), decorating, styling spaces and snooping into numerous homes in Paris, because interior aesthetics have become integral to my new life here. I will explain how I've harnessed a Parisian approach to living and interior design, looking at not just the aesthetics, but also how Parisians use their homes; considering their design ethos and day-to-day domestic style. I will look at the items and furniture pieces that inspire a Parisian's interior aesthetic, and talk about how you can introduce more of this charm into your own surroundings. I'll talk to friends and experts who have been kind enough to give me their interior decorating tips, such as Sarah Poniatowski and Eugénie Trochu. Later on in the section, I will interview a few Parisians whose interior tastes I admire and wouldn't mind emulating in my own space, such as influencer and fashion consultant Géraldine Boublil, who has created an elegant, but comfortable space for herself and her family thanks to a few key iconic items, complemented by candles, flowers and a mixture of textures. Influencer and plant aficionado Thibault Charpentier will share his favourite plants for the home, and Clémentine Lévy, founder of Peonies flower studio, will tell us about her favourite blooms.

Moving to Paris

*'Paris is the only place where I feel that I lead
a life that I can call my own'*
Joan Juliet Buck

Since I moved to Paris eight years ago, I have lived in five different apartments (as well as doing a spot of couch-surfing when I was between homes). My interior taste has evolved exponentially over those years thanks to the city, its surroundings and my Parisian friends. My home style has undergone a complete overhaul, as has my wardrobe and beauty regime. The first apartment I moved into was located on the first floor of a building 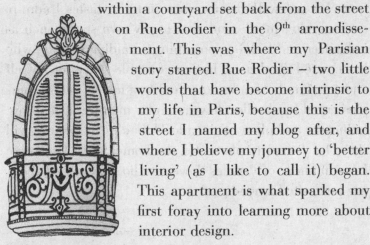 within a courtyard set back from the street on Rue Rodier in the 9th arrondissement. This was where my Parisian story started. Rue Rodier – two little words that have become intrinsic to my life in Paris, because this is the street I named my blog after, and where I believe my journey to 'better living' (as I like to call it) began. This apartment is what sparked my first foray into learning more about interior design.

In the January of 2013, after packing up my life in London and buying a one-way ticket to Paris, I moved into the apartment with my then-boyfriend, the man I'd moved to Paris for. The flat on Rue Rodier wasn't what I would describe as a 'classically Parisian' space. It came fully furnished, and by the time I moved in, my ex had done nothing to add his own personal touch. Our tastes differed wildly (like our opinions and, in the end, our overall compatibility). He, too, was an expat (from Portugal) and had moved to the city for his career, but unbeknownst to me, was already plotting his escape. The apartment came with his job, and I did my best with what I had, but I was fighting a losing battle against the poorly lit, dark-wooden-floored space, which had ugly built-in smoky-mirrored sliding door wardrobes and a distinct lack of pretty features and furniture (apart from the baby blue Smeg fridge that had been installed in the kitchen). As I've said, it wasn't what I would label a 'typical' Parisian apartment: these are to be found in Paris's traditional Haussmannian buildings, and usually come with high ceilings, parquet flooring and fireplaces. It had probably been stripped of its original features and modernised to give it that 'contemporary expat vibe'. It seemed designed to appeal mainly to men (I'm over-generalising, of course), or someone who would spend long days in an office, and whose home life would revolve around eating a takeaway in front of a super-sized TV before crashing into bed. Its function wasn't to be a home, but to be somewhere to sleep and eat between days at work.

Yet I tried as best I could to make it a home for me (and for him). It was my first real experience of attempting to decorate an entire space as an adult, as previously I had always lived in shared accommodation. I pinned images on Pinterest, devoured interiors sites and blogs, began following accounts on Instagram and started learning about how Parisians decorate their homes. I moved furniture around, installed rugs, bought a desk, purchased cushions for the sofas and hung prints. I asked him to put up shelves in the kitchen so I could display cookbooks and place plants. These were all attempts to make the apartment look more lived-in and personalised. Sadly, after a year of living together, we broke up and I moved out. But having already given up my life in London to move to a new city for love, I was not sold on the idea of going back to the UK with my proverbial tail between my legs. Plus a new relationship was blossoming – between me and my new home, Paris. Despite the difficulty of the situation I found myself in – with little work, limited French and now no home, I was determined to stay, boyfriend or no boyfriend. I was incredibly fortunate that a French friend and her partner took me in and I slept on a blow-up bed in their dining room for a month while I looked for a place to live. Flat-hunting in Paris is an experience, to say the least. I visited dozens of apartments, often taking a friend along with me for moral support. More often than not, we'd turn up along with a group of five or six others, all of whom were French and were clutching dissertation-like dossiers that included a work contact, signed guarantor agreement, references from previous landlords, evidence of their last three payslips, bank documents, etc. I rarely got a look in, what with being foreign, freelance and having no one who could act as my guarantor in France.

Now, this is something that you don't discover until you try to find somewhere to live in the French capital: it is extremely difficult to secure an apartment in Paris. Even for Parisians. This is mainly because the tenants have more rights than the owners, and therefore landlords are extremely stringent and careful about whom they rent their properties to. For example, landlords cannot evict tenants in the classic sense – and certainly not during the winter months. So one could live rent-free for a few months, if one so dared. Six years down the line, during my most recent *chasse* (hunt for a flat), in the January of 2020, a friend would tell me: 'You can't claim that you really live in Paris unless you've experienced flat-hunting here.' The implication was that it is some sort of rite of passage that I'd have to go through before I could call myself a true Parisienne. She's right, of course, and it's one of the reasons why interiors and making a space a home are so integral to *la vie Parisienne*. Looking for an apartment in Paris is like searching for a pot of gold at the end of a rainbow: both are equally elusive. Once you find something, you rarely leave – unless, as in my experience, you have to.

Paris was becoming the city where I was growing into myself and finding my way – hardship and challenge

can do that to you – but I still had a lot of lessons to
learn. They say never go back, but of course I did. Once
I'd installed myself in a studio on Rue du Temple in Le
Marais, I started seeing my ex-boyfriend again, after just
a few months apart. Long story short, we planned to
move in together once more. This time, it would be in
a mutual space that we chose together: a blank canvas
that we (more me) could decorate and turn into a home.
Perhaps this was the key to renewing our relationship, I
thought. Maybe the problem wasn't *us*, but the space we
had been living in. We house-hunted all over Paris. This
time, I relished it, because with his solid dossier, thanks
to his full-time employment, we had a better chance of
securing a good place.

Just as I was beginning to get tired of looking (we visited a *lot* of apartments, much to my initial delight and
then fatigue), I happened upon an advert on Le Boncoin
(a popular site for finding apartments and vintage wares,
a bit like Gumtree or Craig's List). From what I could see
from the photos, this was a beautiful fourth-floor apartment in a typical Haussmannian building on Boulevard
de Magenta in the 10th arrondissement – the trendier,
younger and more boho neighbourhood of Paris, which
was top of my list for areas to live in. It was within walking distance of Le Marais and the cool Canal Saint Martin
with its cafés, Asian restaurants (my favourite being a
Korean fusion eatery called SAaM) and caves à vin. In
summer, Parisians on either side of the canal host picnics,
wiling away balmy evenings in a chilled out, happy haze,

surrounded by friends. It's like one big summer festival that you don't need a ticket for.

It wasn't just about the area the apartment was in, though. It was the light that got me. Rays of sunshine streamed in through the huge floor-to-ceiling windows of the large living area, bathing it in light. I was in love. When you know, you know. And I knew I had to live there. I believe that spaces and interiors give off energy, and this was giving it off by the bucket load. It had all the details I was looking for: parquet flooring, high ceilings, a marble fireplace with a huge mirror, ceiling mouldings and cornices. The bedroom, bathroom and kitchen were a little shabby and needed work, but I didn't care, I had my Parisian features. The windows opened on to little wrought-iron balconies, on to which friends would later squeeze themselves to smoke during warm nights when they gathered at our place for drinks and dancing. We'd put the world to rights, while gazing out over the huge trees that lined the boulevard towards the Place Jacques Bonsergent and beyond.

Once we had moved in, I would often stand on those balconies, for no particular reason other than because I *could*. (Despite being known for them, balconies, ones that you can actually stand on or fit a small table on are a rare breed in Paris, with only a couple of floors having them.) I would lean over the iron railings like Shakespeare's Juliet summoning her Romeo, or like a queen in her castle surveying her subjects – 'You there, fetch me a baguette! And you, bring me the butteriest croissant you can find.' Sometimes I would gaze wistfully over the grey-blue rooftops of the adjacent Haussmannian buildings towards Place de la République, a large square created in 1811, where a huge, 9.5 m-high bronze statue of a woman stands centre stage. This is Marianne, who bears an olive branch and wears a wreath on her head. She is swathed in Romanesque cloth and is surrounded by three statues signifying liberty, equality and fraternity – the three pillars of the French constitution. She stands proud, keeping watch over her neighbours' comings and goings, as I did on my balconies, purveying my little slice of the city for four years. Of course, it wasn't all balconies, baguettes and light, but as apartments go, it was pretty special. I had my Parisian dream, and I threw myself into decorating it.

Settling in

'The extension of the art of dwelling is the art of living'
Charlotte Perriand

As my following grew on my Instagram account and blog, I began attracting jobs that often involved my home. This space was becoming integral to my work. Not only did I spend a lot of time there working, but I also started creating content from it, and so the interior started taking shape. I held dinners, threw parties and hosted friends and family there on the *canapé-lit* (pull-out sofa), fully embracing the Parisian lifestyle at home by creating a cosy space that also made the most of the square footage. I was immensely proud of my Parisian apartment. If my relationship hadn't dissolved for the second and final time, I think I was in danger of becoming a bona fide (albeit Parisian) Martha Stewart. KitchenAid even cast me in a campaign for their newest Mini Mixer, with half the footage filmed in the apartment.

Decorating my apartment was also a kind of therapy as my relationship began to break down for the second time. As the cracks in the walls and ceiling of the 150-year-old apartment grew a little more each year, so, too, did the fissures begin to reappear in our relationship after only months of moving back in together. Try as I might to

179

plaster over them with a new space and surroundings, I knew the end was inevitable. Still, it took me a while to extricate myself. When I finally did, though, I was resolute. In the January of 2018, after another of our arguments, which left me depleted and emotionally exhausted, I said I was done. I mention the breakdown of my relationship not just because it is a large part of my Parisian story and one of the challenges I faced living in a foreign country, but also because the idea of losing my lovely apartment was one of the main things keeping me in the relationship. I'm a homebody (I'm a Taurus) and, if nothing else, I need to have a home I feel secure in. I couldn't fathom losing it. But, once I'd finally reached the end of my tether, neither could I fathom staying in the relationship a minute longer.

A home is more than just a dwelling; it's a reflection of you. This might seem like common sense, but many people see their homes as nothing more than a base. I believe the walls, furniture and objects become an extension of your interests and passions. I have always loved interiors, interior design and poking around in beautiful spaces, but until I moved to Paris, I'd never given much thought to how my surroundings reflected me.

When I first moved to France, with no job or friends, I suddenly found myself spending almost all of my time at 'home'. Upon moving, I learned that I'm very sensitive to the energy of my surroundings and where I am living, which had never really occurred to me before. For me, my interior space has become my haven, a place to which

I can retreat when I need to escape from the hectic world outside. I need to feel not only comfortable, but also calm, and I truly believe that houses and apartments give off vibes and energy. They are like living entities, absorbing the lives of those who inhabit their spaces, especially in a city like Paris, where numerous families and people from all walks of life have lived under the roofs of the old buildings. These buildings tell stories, an aspect of Parisian living that was addressed in the film *Amélie*, when she discovers a former tenant's box of treasures that he hid in the wall as a child. In the same way, one of the things that I've noticed about most of my friend's apartments in Paris is that they use the spaces they live in to tell their own stories. And so, with each space, I have tried to tell mine – and I hope you will try to tell your story in your space, with the help of my tips!

As I've hinted at already, I have always had a penchant for snooping around other people's homes. It's a curiosity that was ignited in me at a young age, when I would go house hunting with my mum, as we moved several times as I was growing up. When I arrived in Paris, I was like a kid in a candy shop. I am still fascinated by the huge wooden entrance doors many buildings here have, painted red, maroon, perhaps a Yves Klein blue or a mint green, each often with their own unique carvings. They are like an entranceway to a whole secret world. Every time I tap in the code and push open one of these heavy doors (with a satisfying creaking sound), then step off the street into a hallway entrance – or, better yet, a courtyard – I get the same feeling I imagine Mary had in Frances Hodgson Burnett's *The Secret Garden* when, for the first time, she pushed open the small wooden door in the wall to reveal the enchanting hidden garden beyond. You never quite know what you're going to find on the other side, and that's part of the magic of living in Paris. I've stepped into incredible courtyards, often hiding a large residence – or *hôtel* as they're called. The experience feels rather like reaching your hand into Mary Poppin's magic bag and pulling out a lamppost. I often step back from the doorway, trying to figure out how the courtyards inside can be so big, when the outside street gives no clues.

Because of this, I always jump at the chance to visit a new friend's home. It's the main reason I started doing home tours for my blog: not just because I was interested in interviewing stylish women who inspired my own outward appearance, but because I also really wanted to see where they lived and how they decorated their homes, as it revealed so much about Parisian life.

I have been lucky enough to visit myriad apartments (and houses). Most of these have been inside grand Haussmannian buildings, but I've also visited studio apartments with low ceilings and wooden beams. Because of the unique architecture in Paris, especially in slightly older, more historical areas like Le Marais, which dates back to the seventeenth century; apartments can be found up winding staircases like rabbit warrens, squirreled away under the eaves. It's what makes the way Parisians live so utterly fascinating to the outside world. For example, a colleague of a friend of mine, who worked for Hermès, used to live in the most incredible apartment in Saint Germain. She showed it to me one morning after the three of us met for breakfast at the iconic café Les Deux Magots on Boulevard Saint Germain. Aside from its dramatic floor-to-ceiling windows, marble fireplaces and wooden floors, its walls were adorned with drawings (graffiti) created by Dora Maar, Picasso's muse and a brilliant artist in her own right. Her artwork had been preserved behind protective Perspex coverings so that her drawings could be displayed forever, like permanent (albeit artistic) flies on the wall, witnessing the comings and goings of their housemates for nearly 100 years.

Another memorable apartment, which I visited for an event, belonged to the founder of the Parisian skincare and beauty brand Sisley, Countess Isabelle D'Ornano. It was like visiting a mini Versailles on steroids, if that's possible, with a sweeping staircase that led up to a first-floor apartment packed with art, tapestries, sculptures, chandeliers, animal-print cushions and taxidermy. Parisian interiors are truly unique and by far one of my favourite things about this city.

When searching for my most recent home, I had a few criteria (as one usually does): besides lots of natural light and a minimum square footage, it also had to be old, and ideally in a Haussmannian building with classic Parisian details. I wanted to 'feel' like I was living

in Paris. Luckily despite some of its shabbiness, the tiny
shower room and almost non-existent kitchen, which I've
learned to live with, my current apartment is exactly what
I was looking for.

Finding my interior style and 'curating' a home

'An interior is the natural projection of the soul'
Coco Chanel

Although I've always had a keen interest in interiors, when I first moved to Paris, my own taste was remarkably unrefined, which goes to show you can just as easily find yours if you think it's lacking. I did, however, have a particular penchant for the Scandi-style aesthetic, perhaps because it's minimal, simple and, in my opinion, easy to replicate. I wanted white walls, a grey sofa, black and white monochrome details: what I think of now as a slightly more clinical approach to decorating. While my colour palette hasn't changed much, it's now less defined by one trend or any one inspira-tion; instead, I've developed my own taste, inspired by

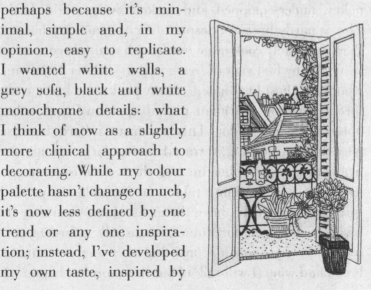

the world around me and reflecting my own interests. I'm more drawn to natural materials and warming textures – think a vintage wooden chair paired with a very design-led modern table –and my taste has evolved to mirror my own personality rather than copying the style of others so outright. Of course, this does come with age, but I honestly don't think I would have developed such a profound sense of interior taste had I not moved to Paris and been surrounded on a daily basis by its beauty and charm.

In a typical Parisian home, it's the living, or family room, which is the heart of the home, unlike in Anglophone homes, where we usually count the kitchen as central to our living space. Unless the apartment has been changed significantly, a Parisian kitchen is usually quite pokey, under-equipped and tucked away at the back. This is partly because, despite the city's culinary history, Parisians rarely cook large meals with multiple courses at home. In my first year of living in Paris, it was mainly me who would host big dinners. At my peak, I cooked a roast for twelve people, a habit picked up from living in big house shares in London. This is a rarity in Paris, because one, there are no big, terraced houses large enough for five or six people to live in; two, there often isn't enough space for a large dining table and multiple chairs; and three, Parisians don't have the inclination. When they do invite friends over for dinner, it's usually a bring-your-own *apéro*-style spread, consisting of cheese, charcuterie, bread and wine (I will talk about this more in chapter 4).

With so many great restaurants and food options on offer, and much of their culinary and social lives spent on terraces, in restaurants and caves à manger, Parisians don't need well-equipped kitchens in their homes. In his book *L'Appart*, a memoir about renovating his apartment in Paris, chef and author David Lebovitz recounts trying to figure out how to install a decent-sized sink in his tiny Parisian kitchen. And it's not just the sinks – unless the kitchen has been redone, you're often lucky if you get any hobs at all! Rental kitchens can be shockingly bare. Unlike in the UK, unfurnished – *non meublé* – really means unfurnished, and you often have to buy your own kitchen appliances, and sometimes even cupboards, too. That's what I've done in my current home: I installed a glass cabinet and hung multiple shelves to give myself kitchen storage. But admittedly there's some charm to be found in tiny, makeshift kitchens. Of course, it could be because of the location, but the idea of making do with what you have and trying to enhance it in creative ways is something I find to be very Parisian. And they do it well. That's something I hope you will take away from this section: permission to step away from the idea of perfection and, instead, harness your interests and inject your own personality into your home. Hang a framed photo of friends on the wall or display a ceramic dish that you picked up while travelling that now holds your jewellery, or fill a gorgeous, sculptural vase with fresh blooms. Curate your home and make it yours.

A chat about interiors with Jackie Kai Ellis

Jackie (@jackiekaiellis) is the bestselling author of *The Measure of My Powers* and the former *pâtisserie* chef and owner of Beaucoup Bakery & Café in Toronto. She bought and renovated an apartment in Paris in 2018. The beautiful first-floor apartment space comes complete with all the features you might expect to find in a Parisian Haussmannian apartment, and when she's not living there, she rents it out to visitors and for photo shoots. As her style is evidently inspired by Paris and beautifully respects the bones of the building, I wanted to chat to her a little bit about her aesthetics.

How would you describe your interior design style?
I like creating balance and interest in contrasting elements – mixing old and new, classic and modern – but, above all, it needs to feel comfortable and liveable.

How did renovating an apartment in Paris inspire your interior taste?
My interior taste was inspired by the apartment's unique architecture: the flooring, fireplaces and ceiling. I would say it offered me the perfect canvas on which to express and play with ideas I had been waiting to create.

How would you describe Parisian interior style?
Typically, I find Parisians enjoy a more modern, minimal aesthetic – one that leans towards Scandinavian, even. I've always thought it was because they had grown up with these old, opulent designs in their grandparents' homes, so much so

that the younger generations want the opposite. Coming from North America, we find charm in classic Haussmannian details and antique furniture found in attics and caves.

What are Parisian interior essentials for you (if one wanted to recreate Parisian style at home)?

Adding things with history and character – a story to tell. Go to *brocantes* or search online and find old, gilded mirrors or an ornately carved bed, and some old, tarnished doorknobs and stained books.

What inspired you to buy and renovate an apartment in Paris?

I was once a designer, and had left this career to study pastry in Paris. The experience changed me, and Paris has been dear to me ever since. Eventually, my career took me all around the world and I found myself craving 'home', so I created one in the city where I discovered the roots of myself.

What are the pros and cons of renovating an apartment in Paris?

The pros are that it's a place of infinite inspiration with many muses, from flea markets to high-end design shops. The main con is that the practical things are not at all practical. For example, it can take six months to get the internet installed.

What are your favourite interior brands?

I love lighting from Studio Henry Wilson, linen bedding from Flax Sleep, alpaca throws from Cadine and ceramics from Janaki Larsen.

What's your favourite piece of furniture in your Parisian apartment, and where did you find it?

My favourite piece in the apartment has to be the vintage armchair I bought myself for my fortieth birthday. I waited for almost a year until I came across the perfect one at KRD, a vintage furniture shop in the 8th arrondissement. It's called the 'Modus armchair' by Illum Wikkelsøe.

The challenges of living in Paris

*'There is but one Paris and however hard living
may be here, and if it became worse and harder
even – the French air clears up the brain and
does good – a world of good'*
Vincent Van Gogh

As I've explained, it's notoriously difficult to find an apartment in Paris. I found my current home, in the 'classic' Parisian way – through a friend of a friend of a friend (*merci*, Phi Phi). After two months of exhaustive searching to no avail, I asked a friend if she knew of anything. She asked her network and, after a week, had found a potential home for me. While it wasn't perfect – there was very little kitchen to speak of, a cupboard-sized shower room and no storage – it had all the classic Parisian details that I was looking for, including wood panelling and two tiny balconies with wrought-iron railings, large enough for potted plants. It was on the fourth floor and had an ample amount of natural light. As I'm sure is clear by now, perfection isn't very Parisian, and I've grown to love its flaws. Unless you have the budget to buy and renovate, one makes do here, finding ways to add charm with ceramics, candles, flowers, prints and books.

There are other negatives that come with living in old Parisian buildings. They often come with cracks in the ceilings and walls, and those walls are thin. You can hear everything – and I mean *everything*. I hardly slept for the first year that I lived in Paris, as I could hear my neighbours' conversations, rows, lovemaking and comings and goings. I have now become accustomed to sleeping with earplugs every night.

Because the streets in Paris are often smaller and tightly packed together, you are closer than you might think to your neighbours living across the street from you. I've often looked out of my window and locked eyes with a neighbour who is looking through theirs at me, or standing on their balcony smoking a cigarette. It leaves me wondering what they might have seen of my private life. Another aspect of these closely packed buildings is the lack of light on the lower floors, making apartments on the third floor and above incredibly sought after. The upside of renting in Paris is that they cannot raise the rents beyond inflation, meaning that they can remain the same for years.

For all the positives that come with living in Paris, there are sacrifices to be made, and one of those is usually square metres. Space really is at a premium in this city, and at times it feels that Parisians live on top of each other. Almost all Parisian homes are apartments – I've only visited one house in the city – which is a far cry from my life in London, where I mainly lived in shared houses with gardens. But Parisians are very good at making the

most of their limited space. In the next section I will outline the interior design lessons that I've learned from the
French, including some about adapting to smaller living
spaces (see page 217).

Ten interior design lessons I've picked up from the Parisians

'The key is for your space not to be too overcharged'
Géraldine Boublil

I'm not a trained interior designer, but I have picked up a thing or two in the eight years that I have been living in Paris. Parisians really know how to create beautiful yet lived-in homes, and I find their interior spaces fascinating and unique, which is one of the reasons I started photo-

graphing friend's homes and doing home tour interviews for my blog. The way that Parisians decorate, isn't really 'decorating' in the traditional sense. They fill their space with things they love, and these things inevitably become the 'decoration'. As Lauren Bastide explains: 'It could be said that "decorating" is a rather poor word to describe the energy many Parisiennes use to turn their homes into cosy, unique little hideaways that they'll struggle to abandon for more than two hours in a row.'

As I said earlier, the beauty of the historical buildings Parisians are surrounded by and live in has undoubtedly influenced their tastes, and they really know how to curate a space. They are highly selective. You won't see a lot of items from IKEA in a Parisian's apartment, for example, and, if you do, they will probably be disguised in some way. And, just like their clothing, they invest in items for their homes that will stand the test of time. Rental contracts here are long and Parisians rarely move unless they have to, so they will inevitably be in their homes for many years. Their taste in interiors goes far beyond clichés, and they don't follow any specific rules, but from browsing websites like The Socialite Family and Milk Decoration as well as happily nosing around other people's homes, I've come to realise that there are a few running themes in the way that Parisians adorn their apartments. Here are the key lessons I've learned.

Pay attention to the details and heed the history

Decorating the Parisian way starts with the building's bones. If you're living in a Haussmannian building, these bones will consist of parquet wood flooring, high ceilings, large windows, wall panelling, ceiling mouldings, and a fireplace or two, if you're lucky. The first thing to learn about decorating the Parisian way is to remain faithful to a space's original features. Highlight them: they should become focal points, as well as a starting block for your interior decoration decisions. If you are lacking in the features department, you could always create them – panelling and mouldings can be fashioned, and fireplaces installed.

Mix old with new

When I moved to Paris, I rather naively thought that I had to stick with a particular trend when it came to interior design, and that if I bought a modern piece of furniture, all the other pieces in the room had to be of the same ilk. A little silly in hindsight, I know, but I thought I had to either like new or old, contemporary or vintage. Living in Paris has taught me that I don't have to make such decisions – or so much effort – and instead I now embrace the effortlessness of Parisian life. It's not meant to be so hard. If it's hard, then maybe it's not right. And I've learned that old looks good with new: a vintage Parisian *buffet* (sideboard) looks great against a modern dining table; a marble-topped vintage bedside table will complement a newly upholstered headboard; and an iconic chair designed by Pierre Jeanneret actually works brilliantly next to a large, contemporary white wardrobe in the bedroom. It's all about finding a balance between old and new.

Make the most of what you've got

This is a lesson that could be related back to the Parisian attitude towards beauty and body image, but it also works for their approach towards interiors – and life in general. Although most Parisian apartments do come with a certain amount of charm and character, they can often be tiny, run-down and poorly lit. But Parisians know how to make the most of what they have. They make do, because the art of Parisian living isn't about being perfect or doing things perfectly. Some of the most interesting spaces I've seen have also been the smallest or most challenging: places where the tenant has completely transformed the interior, adding their unique personal touch to make the most of the small space. This can be done in many ways, such as: using refashioned wooden crates as shelving, filled with books and then topped with plants; placing a sofa at the foot of the bed to create a separate living area; installing a glass-topped coffee table with space inside to display items for a more personal touch; or placing table lamps on surfaces instead of pendant lighting to create a magical and cosy cave-like space that is completely unique.

Ignore trends and take cues from 'effortless' French fashion

In 2017, I contributed to an article about French interior style for US *Elle Décor*. My rule was simple: don't try too hard! And I stand by that. The best way to do this is to keep things simple. Don't overthink it or over-style. This is a rule that we've already seen in the chapters on fashion and beauty, and it also applies to interiors. Parisians like to have homes that feel lived in, despite the beautiful things they house, so don't spend hours agonising over where to place something. Make a quick decision, then refer back to it over the next few days to see how you feel. It's likely that you'll get used to its new setting, and will like it. If it doesn't feel right, you can simply move it later.

Reflect your personality

This is possibly the most important lesson I learned. While you might be inspired by Parisian interiors, try to find your own style. What do *you* like? What are your interests? What makes you tick? If you're not sure where to start, try looking to your wardrobe for inspiration. Many interior designers will suggest this when beginning the interior design process. Looking at the clothes you love can help you decide on the colours you'd like to decorate your home with, for example. If you feel good wearing a particular colour, it's likely that you will feel good having it on your walls or highlighted in little details around your home. Then you can layer on personal items, such as framed photos, favourite books, ceramics, magazines, dried and fresh flowers, that pretty vase you've had your eye on for a while – just as you would layer jewellery and accessories over an outfit.

Curate your home as you would your wardrobe

Be thoughtful with your interior choices. There's no rush – if you're anything like a Parisian, you'll be in your home for a long time. Take your time and carefully

seek out items that reflect you in order to create a beautiful home. There is no such thing as 'finished' when it comes to interior design: your home should evolve with you. Parisian homes are not 'polished': they are an accumulation of things collected and found over the years. Invest in items for your home as you would your wardrobe – choose items that will last and that perhaps one day you can pass down to a family member.

Less is more

I'm aware that this is a running theme throughout this book, but it rings true in many aspects of a Parisian's life. In a busy city like Paris, where it is noisy and you often live on top of each other in old buildings with thin walls, the last thing you want is an overloaded home. If you do have a lot of stuff, good storage is your friend. Better yet, get rid of any excess items that are cluttering up your space (unless, that is, you really like stuff and being surrounded by lots of things doesn't stress you out). Either way, your home should be your sanctuary: a comfortable place in which you can relax.

Invest in good lighting

As I explained earlier, there is often a lack of natural light in Parisian apartments, especially those on lower floors. They can get very dark in winter, especially with *la grisaille Parisienne* (when Paris seems to be grey for days on end). If you're looking for a home in Paris, remember that any apartment below the third floor that doesn't have floor-to-ceiling windows, or that looks out on to a courtyard, will not get a lot of natural light. In fact, most courtyard apartments don't get much natural light full stop, regardless of what floor they're on, so these are worth avoiding if you suffer from SAD, as I do. I learned this the hard way when I lived in the apartment on Rue Rodier in my first year in Paris.

But whether you have a lot of natural light in your apartment or not, good lighting can make all the difference. It not only brightens a space, but also brings warmth and ambience – it can change the energy of a space. I see ceiling lights as more decorative rather than useful: I rarely use the overhead light in my living room, and instead favour floor, wall and table lamps.

Don't save something for best – use it now

Life can be uncertain and precarious, so we should make the effort to enjoy the special things we have. Of course, things break, but beautiful things are there to be used, not hidden away. Parisians have a bit of a 'live and let live' attitude in this regard, as they do in other areas of their lives. It's not that they care less, it's just that they believe life is to be enjoyed, and that means using the 'good' wine glasses on a regular basis rather than avoiding them for fear that they will break! Their home space is to be lived in and the items within it are to be used. If something does get broken or damaged, at least you got some use and enjoyment out of it.

Up-cycle items

Another way of adding personality to your home the Parisian way is to find second-hand and vintage objects and update them. Seek out a lovely new white or pleated lampshade for a lamp base that you found at a market, re-upholster a chair, or reframe an old artwork, print or poster. This is one of the best and easiest ways to put your personal stamp on an item and make your space unique.

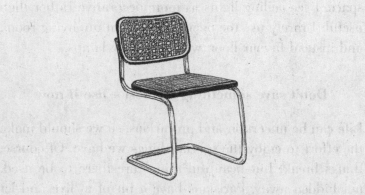

An interiors chat with Géraldine Boublil

Géraldine (@erinoffduty) is an artistic director and consultant working within the fashion and interiors realm. She's also an influencer, with 133,000 followers at the time of writing, and she is co-founder of a new high-end interiors brand called Things From, which she describes as art pieces for the home that marry interior design with fashion. She has one of the most beautifully and artfully curated apartments that I've seen, with a pared-back and minimalist aesthetic. I asked her a bit more about her taste, and for a few tips on how she would create a Parisian-inspired home.

How would you describe your interior aesthetic?
Cosy, quite minimalist, yet warm.
What makes Parisian apartments so unique and enviable?
The Haussmannian style is highly appreciated all over the world. The golden-framed mirrors, the mouldings, the marble chimneys – all these things make Parisian homes totally unique and charming.
Where do you source the pieces in your home from?
I buy ninety per cent of my items vintage and second-hand. Sometimes I source them from *les puces* – I recently purchased some vintage Italian chairs, which I had reupholstered with a Knoll fabric. They look very unique. But it can be quite expensive, and it depends on the day you go. I love *brocantes* such as the one on Rue de Bretagne in the third

arrondissement, and sometimes I find them randomly around Paris. I also love shopping for interior items in Copenhagen, which is the place I often dream of buying things, but it's too far and too expensive to ship from, as is the Rose Bowl flea market in Los Angeles. I also sometimes buy online from vintage interior sites such as Selency. Otherwise, I will have things made. I love Louise Roe lamps and objects, and occasionally steal from my dad's collection of sixties and seventies interior pieces.

Where do you draw your interior design inspiration from?

My parents bought their first home from a French architect in 1978. It's located just outside Paris, near Versailles. He sold them the majority of his beautiful furniture, too. I lived in this environment for eighteen years, and it clearly inspired the interior taste that I have today.

What is your favourite design piece at home?

A seventies Italian-style lacquer table that looks like marble.

What's your favourite place in Paris?

Toraya is my favourite place for lunch or teatime. My favourite walk is dropping my daughter off at school on the Left Bank, then walking back across La Concorde Bridge.

Géraldine's interior design tips

1. Can't find what you're looking for? Design it yourself and have it made.

I have been looking for the perfect dining table for the past two years, and I couldn't find it, so I decided to find someone to make it for me. I'm also having a transparent shelving system made for the living room, because I didn't want to cover up the beautiful mouldings in there.

2. Style up your shelving

I style my shelving with a few books arranged in different ways – some standing up, others lying down. Then I style the rest of the shelving with objects from my travels and candles – but always a small quantity of objects. The key is for the shelving not to be overly full.

3. Incorporate round and smooth shapes throughout your home

I'm a big believer in Feng Shui and allowing energy to flow within a space (for example, I would never put anything under my bed). I think the best way to do this is to incorporate round and smooth shapes within your home – I don't like sharp corners, which can block the energy. For example, my couch is in the shape of a wave, and all my lighting fixtures are round. These shapes also create a continuity with the circular mouldings of my Parisian apartment.

Items that will instantly add Parisian charm to any space

'A Parisian apartment is sophisticated without being flashy or pretentious. There's a reason that we say "chic à la française". I think there is a soul and authenticity to it'
Charlotte Cadé, co-founder of Selency

If you're reading this book, the chances are that you love Paris and admire the Parisian lifestyle, and therefore perhaps you'd like to know how to emulate Parisian style in your own home. While, as I've said, it can be hard to define their style exactly, there are a few key pieces that most Parisian homes have. I'm not going to tell you to go out and buy a Marie Antoinette-style bed. (Of course you can do so if you wish, but like the beret, it can look a little dated and take things a little too far on the stereotype spectrum.) Instead, I'm going to talk about a few pieces that I personally love and have found in many of my Parisian friends' homes.

A decorative mirror

The focal point of a room in a Parisian home is usually a fireplace and, above that, there will often be a large mirror. These beautiful, ornate mirrors came into use in the eighteenth century, when having one of these in your home was a sign of wealth. They remain a timeless decorative item that has never gone out of style. There are two main types of Parisian mirrors. First up, the Trumeau, which is a wall mirror that was originally made in France in the second half of the eighteenth century. Its name comes from the French word *trumeau*, which means the space in between two windows. The mirror is set into a larger wooden frame, which usually has a sculptural decoration at the top. The second style is the Louis Philippe, which is much less ornate and moving towards minimal (for Paris). This style comes from the mid-nineteenth century, when King  Louis Philippe ruled from 1830–48. These mirrors have a thick, rectangular frame with curved edges at the top, and were originally finished in gold or silver leaf.

If you don't have a fireplace to hang your mirror above, place it behind the sofa on a shelf, or above a console table or *buffet*. You can, of course, opt for a frame with much less fuss, but either way, mirrors in a living room are very Parisian and help give the illusion of more space.

You can find these types of mirrors online – try Selency and Le Boncoin from Paris, or visit *les puces* (flea markets), although they can be more expensive. A few high-street brands have begun replicating them, too; I actually picked up mine from Zara!

Where to find them: second-hand on sites like Gumtree, Selency and Le Boncoin (both in France), Facebook Marketplace, Anthropologie, Oka

Candles

Candles are not just for Christmas. I say this because I generally used to associate candles with the holiday season and would rarely light them during the rest of the year. But beautiful candles are a staple in a Parisian's home, which is no surprise considering Paris birthed two of the world's most beautiful candle brands. The first is Diptyque, which you probably already know of – you might even have one of their candles in your home right now, and I've already talked about their fragrances (see page 156). The other is Cire Trudon, the oldest candle-maker in the world – I'll talk about this brand more on page 222. You can mix candles in glass holders along with pillar and taper candles in different shapes and sizes.

Favourite brands: Diptyque, Jo Malone London, Annick Goutal, Cire Trudon

A sculptural ceramic or cut-glass vase

One thing you will surely find in a Parisian's home is a vase filled with flowers. We love our florists in Paris, and a little like the *boulangeries*, there is more than one in every neighbourhood. During lockdown, I loved nothing more than buying a bunch of fresh blooms weekly; it was one of the simple pleasures that kept me going during this difficult period. Flowers can instantly lift a room, and having a lovely vase to house them in is just as important as the blooms them-selves. I'd advise you to own a few vases if you can. They don't need to be expensive – you can pick up some lovely options on the high street or second-hand, for example – but this is an item worth investing in. Opt for cut-glass or a neutral colour for a homeware piece that won't go out of fashion.

Favourite brands: Anissa Kermiche, MENU, Louise Roe, HK Living, Iittala x Alvar Aalto, Hay, Simone Bodmer-Turner, Fferrone Design and Tom Dixon, vintage (Selency, LeBonCoin, eBay)

Glassware

If you didn't already know, Parisians love good wine (and I'll be talking about that in chapter 4). What better way to drink it than out of a beautiful glass? I've started collecting glassware in recent years, as I think it looks beautiful on display as well as on the table and in your hand.

Favourite brands: Louise Roe, Ferm Living, Serax, R+D.LAB, Bitossi, Iittala, LSA International, Saint-Louis Crystal, vintage

The iconic chair

A key feature in a Parisian home is an iconic chair. Think the white bouclé Pierre Paulin F598 chair in the home of Leia Sfez, the pair of mid-century upholstered chairs in Géraldine Boublil's home, or my own replica of the Pierre Jeanneret 'easy chair' created by Srelle, which was one of the first pieces that I acquired for my new apartment last year when I moved in. Jeanneret was a Swiss architect and designer, who collaborated heavily with his cousin, the better-known designer and architect Le Corbusier. But one of Jeanneret's claims to fame is his range of wicker and wood furniture pieces, which he designed and produced for public buildings in the city of Chandigarh, India. Other designs to look out for are the Eames lounge chair and ottoman, the Pacha Lounge Chair by Pierre

Paulin for Gubi, the Warner Platner chair for Knoll, the Wassily chair by Marcel Breuer, the LCW chair by Ray and Charles Eames, and the Togo chair by Ligne Roset.

Favourite brands: Thonet, Srelle, Ligne Roset, Pierre Paulin

Fresh flowers

Peonies have made a name for themselves in Paris thanks to Instagram. As soon as spring hits, they are the main flower you will see in markets, florists and in the arms of Parisians. I, for one, certainly start picking them up from my local florist in May. But fresh flowers are a regular sight in Parisian homes all year round – just look at Jeanne Damas's photos on Instagram (@jeannedamas) and at artist Nina Koltchitskaia's beautiful account (@ninakolchitskaia) – fresh blooms are daily residents in her home and inspiration for her artworks.

Favourite florals: peonies, dahlias, Ranunculus, tulips, roses, stocks

A Berber rug

Parisian apartments are rarely, if ever, carpeted – why cover up that beautiful parquet flooring? But Parisians do like to add rugs for cosiness and warmth. One design I've seen time and time again, and even owned myself at some point), is the Berber rug. The Parisians have a bit of an affinity with Morocco, and it's one of their main travel destinations. This is partly due to their historical ties – after France conquered Algeria in 1844, they tried to take Morocco, and the Franco-Moroccan War broke out. They didn't succeed, but the country became a French Protectorate in 1912 through the Treaty of Fez –and due to the fact that French is Morocco's second language, making it an easy place for Parisians to visit. Plus, of course, it has a rich and colourful culture. Visiting Parisians will often bring back ceramics and other knick-knacks, but the Berber rug is the most prolific Moroccan item in the capital's homes. Whether you go for cream with a diagonal pattern or a colourful version, a rug of this style will add instant Parisian charm and a cosy vibe to your living space.

Favourite brands: Beldy Paris, LRNCE, AM.PM, Nordic Knots

Dried flowers

I mentioned that Parisians love fresh blooms, but they also have a weakness for dried flowers (just look at Sabina Socol's apartment on Instagram – @sabinasocol), and it's rare that you'll find a Parisian home without them. I was, incidentally, included in a *Glamour UK* article about Parisian homes featuring dried flowers. Plus, of course, the advantage of a dried bunch is that they don't die, so you can keep them for as long as you like.

Plants

With the lack of gardens (and often balconies) for growing plants, having greenery inside an apartment is not only key for health reasons, but also for bringing a bit of nature into the home. Later, I'll share some advice from my friend and plant expert Thibault Charpentier on the best plants for your home – see page 220.

Books & Coffee table books

Another item that you will find plenty of in a Parisian's home are books. They are big readers and love to display their books on coffee tables, in corners or beside the bed. Sometimes stacks of books even take on the role of furniture, becoming impromptu side tables or plant stands.

Favourite coffee table magazines:
House and Garden, World of Interiors, Vogue, Harpers Bazaar, Apartamento, Holiday, Wallpaper, Cereal, Kinfolk.

Favourite coffee table books: *Live Beautiful* by Athena Calderone,

Architectural Digest at 100, *Eat Drink Nap* by Soho House, *The Kinfolk Table*, *This is Home: The Art of Simple Living* by Natalie Walton, *Painting Beyond Pollock* by Morgan Falconer and any of the books from Assouline.

Art & prints

As I've already said, living in a city like Paris undoubtedly enhances your eye for aesthetics, as it does your appreciation of all things artistic, including culture, art and literature. So one thing you will certainly find in a Parisian home are artworks, prints, vintage posters and sculptures – even framed taxidermy, as Eugénie Trochu revealed when I spoke to her (see page 225).

Favourite brands: The Poster Club, Curated Copenhagen, LNRC, Deyrolle

Clémentine Lévy's favourite flowers for the home

Clémentine (@clementinelevy) founded the first flower café, Peonies Paris, in 2016. She has since closed up shop following the coronavirus pandemic, but is now hosting flower-arranging workshops and creating a new project, Peonies School & Garden. Here, she shares her three favourite flowers that she loves to display in the home.

My three favourite flowers are the Julia Rose peony, the Butterfly ranunculus and the Koko Loko rose. I love pastel flowers: they offer exactly the kind of palette I'm excited to work with. For those new to flower arranging, it's also an easy palette to start with, as it's very difficult to go wrong when mixing pastel hues. Each of these flowers are also very pretty on their own: you can have only one in a small bud vase, displayed on a nice dinner table, and it will create a very simple but beautiful centre piece.

Julia Rose peonies only bloom once a year, at the end of May until the end of June. This hybrid was created by Toichi Itoh and comes from Japan.

Butterfly ranunculus bloom throughout spring and are also from Japan. Sadly, they are quite difficult to find in the shops.

Koko Loko roses bloom from May until the end of October. They are usually good to buy from spring until the end of autumn.

Practising Parisienne

All of these flowers like water, but not too much – fill the vase just a third full, and always give the stems a nice diagonal cut with clean, sharp scissors before you place them into the water.

How to style a small space, the Parisian way

As I've said, twenty-square-metre studio apartments are commonplace in Paris. I lived in one for six months in Le Marais, and I have friends who call them home. My last 'apartment', although not technically a studio, was a mere thirty-two square metres. The upside of all these studios and small spaces is that there are a lot of them in Paris, and so it's an easier city in which to find a home for one. The downside, of course, is that they can be tiny! I've visited 'apartments' as shockingly small as seventeen square metres. But there are ways that one can make the most of small-space living, and the Parisians are experts at this. So here are a few of my tips.

Add a big mirror – I've already explained that big mirrors are a key feature in Parisian homes, but in a small apartment they serve an extra purpose, immediately giving the illusion of more space. Hang one above your sofa, bed or a console table. You could also add a floor-length mirror near your front door, or even hang one on the back of it.

Create zones with furniture – Just because your bed is in the same area as your living space, doesn't mean you can't create a *salon* with a sofa and coffee table. The best way to do this is by adding a rug under your coffee table and sofa to help create the illusion that this is in fact a separate space. If you have the square footage for it, you could also use an open-backed bookcase to separate your sleeping area from your living space.

If you don't have space for both a bed and sofa, invest in a good sofa bed – I have friends who have slept on sofa beds for a couple of years when living in a studio. There are some very good sofa beds on the market now.

Get clever with storage – A large wardrobe, preferably the same colour as your walls, is one of the most useful pieces you can invest in. Even though it will take up space, it will help keep your floors tidy. Use storage solutions such as drawer separators to keep your smaller clothing items, such as underwear and socks in order. Tylko are a great brand who make made-to-measure storage systems.

Put up shelves – Not only will this give you more storage and help keep your floors clear, it will also give you surface space to style your favourite objects.

Play with colour – I'd generally go for white in a small space in order to allow as much natural light as possible to bounce off the walls. But sometimes a darker colour can create depth. Plus, in a studio apartment, you can use different colours to create the illusion of a separate bedroom and living area, for example, painting the wall behind the bed a different colour.

Get a *lit coffre* (lift-up bed) or a bed with drawers – These will cost more than a standard bed, but it's worth the investment as it can save you space and give you lots of extra storage. I have one from BoConcept.

Opt for cabinets with doors rather than open shelving – If you really are tight on space, hiding things away behind doors will give the illusion of more room. Too many things on display will make your home look over-crowded.

Curate your space – As ever, be selective with the items you display. After all, your home is there to tell your story.

Thibault Charpentier's indoor plant recommendations

Parisians like to bring greenery and nature into their homes as they rarely have gardens, so I asked my friend, photographer and plant aficionado, Thibault (@plantes_daddy) for his top recommendations for easy-to-care-for indoor plants.

Zamioculcas zamiifolia or the 'ZZ plant'

This is a tropical perennial plant native to eastern Africa and part of the *Araceae* family. It likes low levels of light, so it's best to avoid direct sunlight, and it can last weeks without watering – in fact, too much water can cause stem rot. Allow the top of the soil to become dry to the touch between watering. You can water as little as once a month in colder weather. I love this plant because it has beautiful, rich, glossy green leaves, plus it's easy to care for and is happy in the darker corners of your home.

Calathea zebrina or the 'Zebra plant'

This is an award-winning species in the *Marantaceae* family, and is native to southeastern Brazil. It won the Royal Horticultural Society's Award of Garden Merit. This is a beautiful, graphical plant and it, too, likes the shade, so it's perfect for our interiors. It doesn't need much water, but if you forget, it will let you know in a dramatic fashion – all its leaves will roll up, and then drop like they're dead. Once watered, the leaves will straighten up again, like magic!

Interiors & home life

Spathiphyllum or the 'Peace lily'

This is a monocotyledonous flowering plant, also in the
Araceae family, and native to tropical regions of the Americas
and Southeast Asia. Small varieties look attractive on a tabletop,
while bigger ones can occupy a nice-sized spot on the floor.
They filter more pollutants than most other plant species, so
are great for the bedroom. This plant is also very dramatic when
thirsty, so don't worry if you forget to water it – it will definitely
remind you. As with the zebra plant, the leaves will straighten
up again once watered to thank you! I love this plant because it
is very easy to care for and the 'Sensation' variant – the largest
in the species – makes a real statement in a room.

Iconic French homeware brands to know

Astier de Villatte

Despite its antique aesthetic, Astier de Villatte was only founded in 1996. It has since become a go-to brand for the ceramics and candles that are synonymous with a classical Parisian style. Their white handmade designs are inspired by curiosities from the eighteenth and nineteenth centuries, and the brand's founders, Benoît Astier de Villatte and Ivan Pericoli, along with their team of ceramicists, make their creations in the same workshop that used to create Napoleon's silver. Their unique ceramic pieces are instantly recognisable as French, so if you want to infuse a bit of traditional Parisian charm into your space without changing too much, these are just the ticket. But as Eugénie Trochu said when I spoke to her (see page 225), it would be over the top to have a lot of items from them – so invest in just a couple, such as a vase or incense holder.

Cire Trudon

As I mentioned on page 208, Cire Trudon are the oldest candlemakers in the world. The brand was founded in 1643 during the reign of Louis XIV, and creates seductive scents in glass casing – you'll recognise them by the decorative gold crest on the front of the glass holders. They also hand-produce the most beautifully ornate candles inspired by busts of Marie Antoinette and Napoleon. I was lucky enough to be invited to their factory in Normandy last summer to see first-hand how the candles are made. They adhere to old traditions, so although the candles can be pricey, you know you are buying a piece of true craftsmanship. I particularly love their rose-coloured Marie Antoinette busts, which would look great on a mantelpiece.

Saint-Louis Crystal
The French crystal brand dates back a staggering five centuries. It was first founded in 1586 as Muntzthal Glassworks, but in 1767 it became the *Verrerie Royale*, meaning Royal Glassworks, by order of the then-king, Louis XV. Since 1829, the brand has been known as Cristallerie Royale de Saint-Louis, or just Saint-Louis, and is devoted to the production of crystal glass pieces that marry tradition with art deco and art nouveau design. Today, they also make more minimal creations, and many Parisians will go to them to invest in a set of wine or champagne glasses that they intend to have forever.

Puiforcat
Puiforcat is a Parisian silversmith brand that has been creating iconic, intricately designed and often engraved table services and cutlery from sterling silver since 1820, another example of unique Parisian craftsmanship that

has stood the test of time. I was also fortunate enough to join them in Beijing in China for the launch of their new sommelier collection in 2017. Their pieces are pricey but timeless, and make unique mementos and gifts.

Eugénie Trochu's favourite three pieces and places for interiors shopping

Eugénie is now Head of Editorial Content for *Vogue Paris*. While her speciality is style, she also looks after the home tours for Vogue.fr and she has created an eclectic and colourful space in her Parisian apartment, so I wanted to find out a bit more about her favourite pieces. More recently, she launched a new Instagram account called @gooodspot, where she posts about fashionable tips and covetable lifestyle and interiors brands.

My favourite three pieces in my home

1. **An old map of South America.**

   This is a trip that I'd like to do in the not-too-distant future. I think it's cool to have a map on a wall. This is an old-school map that I found at the Village Saint Paul in Paris. I don't know the date, but it's my parents' generation. I like to fill my walls, and maps are great for this. Everything that's on my walls is very important to me.

2. **My record player**

   I keep records next to it, which I think adds a nice visual touch. It's a Pro-ject, which is the best brand of record players. Mine's the entry-level price, as the brand is expensive. It was a present from friends three years ago. It's a lovely object, and displaying the records adds colour to the apartment. My place isn't very big, so I've thought carefully about everything that I have on display and I play with the decoration.

3. **An old trunk**

I found this at a *brocante* near my parents' place in Normandy. Essentially, I have old things at my place – they come from different places and give the impression of travel.

Three of my favourite places in Paris for interiors shopping

1. **Sabre Paris**

They create tableware, producing a lot of beautiful pieces including fun and often whimsical, colourful and patterned cutlery that helps to dress your table. For example, some come with handles in the shape of bamboo. And the prices are affordable.

www.sabreparis.fr
4 Rue des Quatre Vents, 75007

2. **La Cabane de l'Ours**

They sell blankets and cushions with Native American prints in the spirit of Pendleton. I covered my white sofa in them as it's no longer white . . . There used to be a boutique in Paris, but now it's only online.

www.lacabanedelours.com

3. **Deyrolle Taxidermy**

This is a well-known place for taxidermy, and has been around since 1831. They have lots of stuffed animals there, and on the first floor they have butterflies. I personally love taxidermy butterflies. You can create your own composition and choose to have it displayed in a glass bell jar or framed. I chose to have a gold scarab beetle and three butterflies framed.

www.deyrolle.com

46 Rue du Bac, 75007

How to create a cosy & comfortable living space the Parisian way

'Comfortable' and 'cosy' are two adjectives that I've always associated with Parisian spaces. Incidentally, they are also key words for 2021's interior design trends, according to an article that was published in *US Vogue* at the beginning of the year. Of course, Parisians have an uncanny knack for staying ahead of the trends, even if they themselves don't necessarily follow them. So how can you create a cosy space the Parisian way? Here are a few easy ways.

Layer textures – I've already talked about the Berber rug (page 211), which is a popular way of creating a cosy space you'll never want to leave. Add wool and cashmere throws to the sofa, and even a floor cushion, to soften and enhance your space.

A comfy sofa – Invest in a sofa that you can sink into, preferably in linen or wool bouclé and, ideally, as Géraldine pointed out in her tips, one with curved edges, for a cosier interior.

Candles – Candles are instant cosy-creators and mood-enhancers. Light a few – one scented, plus several long, tapered candles in glass, ceramic or wooden holders.

Sarah Poniatowski's tips for using colour in the home

Sarah (@sarahponiatowski) is the founder of Maison Sarah Lavoine. Her bold use of primary colours is instantly recognisable, and has helped define her as one of Paris's most sought-after designers and brands for the home. From her striped lampshades to her candles and colourful cushions, she has created a range of items that instantly add a bit of unique modern Parisian charm into a space. I asked her for her tips for using colour in the home.

Investigate!

The starting point for every colour project is the soul of the place and its natural light. Places with history talk. Find out when the building was built, and why. For whom and by whom was it built? What is its geographical context? Think about the surrounding nature, its orientation, and the rhythm of the sun over twenty-four hours and through the seasons. The smallest detail, such as the coloured motif of an original tile or the remains of some wallpaper, can become the source of chromatic inspiration. It is a question of going in the direction of a building's history while simultaneously modernising your space.

Assert your personality

What colours appeal to you? Trust yourself and make your space your own. Let your interests and desires speak. It's the hardest part, but try to detach yourself from current interior trends to create a personal and timeless story.

Create harmony within each room

Have fun! The different rooms of your home allow for various areas of expression. Each piece has its own character and its own signature. But be sure to keep a certain stylistic consistency to avoid going all over the place. The materials that accompany the colours in your project are a good common thread. The right choice of flooring is essential because, together with the walls, the floors anchor the personality of the décor.

Choose your paint finishes

A paint finish can reflect more or less light. You can play with different paint finishes to liven up a room:

- A matte finish absorbs light; it is therefore ideal for restoring colours and for concealing irregularities in a material.
- A velvety satin finish is less fragile, so it is best for bathrooms, hallways and children's rooms.
- A shiny lacquer finish is like a mirror. It creates a lot of depth and it reflects light, giving a feeling of infinity.

How to shop vintage for your home and what to look for

There's something liberating (and empowering, I might add) about finding a unique vintage piece of furniture or homeware. And it's not just about the thrill of the hunt: that moment when someone asks you where it's from and you can answer confidently, 'It's vintage' is equally satisfying. Even better if it was a bargain. Thrifting and buying vintage and second-hand is also the best way to put your signature and personal stamp on a space. I've learned a lot about buying vintage and second-hand since living in Paris, and have picked up some unique treasures that I know I'll take with me into my future homes.

Of course, IKEA and the likes of Habitat and Made. com have their merits, and I've found some lovely pieces in all three, but there's just something so satisfying about finding a rare piece of homeware or furniture that no one else has. Plus, if it's a sought-after piece, it won't lose its value. It's the same feeling I get when I wear a piece of vintage clothing. These items add more personality, colour and vibrancy to a home, in a way that a piece of new, mass-produced furniture never will. They tell a story, and Parisians love nothing more than telling stories with their homes. I've spent numerous weekends browsing *brocantes* and searching online for unique pieces for my home, and I have learned a few lessons that I hope will make your hunt easier, but no less thrilling.

Do your research – Nothing beats being prepared when you start to buy vintage or second-hand. Buy books and read magazines. A few of my favourite books are: *This is Home* by Natalie Walton; *Maison: Parisian Chic At Home* by Inès de La Fressange and Marin Montagut; *Live Beautiful* by Athena Calderone and *Interiors Now* series by Taschen. As for magazines, look at *House & Garden*, *Architectural Digest*, *Domino*, *House Beautiful*, *Milk Magazine* and *World of Interiors*. You can also browse websites, like Dwell, My Domaine, Mad About the House and, of course, Instagram. Before you start searching (and hunting) in real life, it's good to know what you're looking for. Cut out images and create mood boards, or pin them to your Pinterest page.

Set up email alerts – If you're searching online, set up alerts and be specific with words – see my list of vocabulary on page 234.

Don't be afraid to negotiate – I've picked up some great bargains just by being a bit bolder in my negotiations. Most second-hand sellers will expect you to haggle a little bit. I always knock off more than I would ultimately be willing to pay, as a seller will always negotiate up and this gives you more room to manoeuvre financially, meaning you will (hopefully!) end up paying almost exactly what you wanted to from the beginning.

Customise items yourself – Found a lamp base, but don't like the shade? You can easily change it – and it won't necessarily cost much. Look on Etsy for examples of pleated lampshades, one of my favourite styles of shade. Habitat sell neutral linen versions for low prices, as do H&M. There have been quite a few designers and brands that have started creating unique lampshades recently, such as Matilda Goad, who makes gorgeous, scalloped styles.

Be patient – Finally, patience is golden when it comes to the search for something unique. You are curating your home, so you want to populate it with pieces that you are going to love for years to come. And it'll be worth the wait when you find a great piece to treasure.

What to look for – Anything made from marble; glass, crystal, metal and even wood candleholders; alabaster lamp bases (as I said, you can always add the lampshade later); glass and ceramic vases; tableware and glassware; iconic chairs; mid-century furniture, such as console tables and *buffets*; female busts; and all kinds of ceramics.

Where to buy vintage online

— 1stdibs
— Selency
— eBay
— Le BonCoin

— Etsy
— In the UK, you can also try panomo.com, preloved. co.uk and gumtree.com

> ✤ **TOP TIP** ✤
>
> As I do with wardrobe items I'm currently coveting, create wish lists for items you want to keep an eye out for. Most sites will have this option.

✤

French vocabulary

Chiner – literally means 'to bargain-hunt'

Brocantes – flea markets or markets selling second-hand goods. In Paris, a *brocante* is usually a vintage or antiques market of higher-quality goods: these are not necessarily the places for finding a bargain. *Brocantes* are better in smaller towns and villages.

Marché des puces – flea markets (*puce* means 'flea')

An interiors chat with Charlotte Cadé

Charlotte (@charlotte_selency) has a passion for interiors and bargain-hunting that inspired her to co-found Selency, an online vintage marketplace. When we chatted, she told me that her hobby had become too time-consuming, and she'd thought, wouldn't it be great to have a site that was a collection of all the best second-hand places: a modern *brocante* that was also a service? Selency was born in 2014 and it has since become France's number-one destination for vintage furniture and accessories.

How would you describe Parisian interior style?

I would say that a Parisian apartment is sophisticated, without being flashy or pretentious. There's a reason why we say *chic à la française*. I think there is a soul and authenticity to it, too. Another characteristic of Parisian interior design is a mix of styles and eras.

What are the Parisian interior essentials?

No matter the size of the apartment, there's always a coffee table, because we often eat off it – it's part of the Parisian lifestyle, as we spend a lot of the time in the living room. Then there will obviously be a sofa, and perhaps a couple of armchairs, to create an environment where we feel good. We try to create an interior that reflects the person living in the apartment: their way of living and their interests.

What are some current Parisian interior trends?

Natural fibres and materials are making a big comeback: cane and rattan are in vogue right now, along with anything that has an authentic style and a simple design, inspired by the creations of Charlotte Perriand, for example. Cut glass has also become very popular, such as glass decanters for whisky, as have unframed mirrors with an atypical shape.

What are your favourite brands or designers?

I'm not really attached to any one designer in particular. I do like Charlotte Perriand – she's very inspiring – but what I really like is diversity. That's what I like about *brocantes* or Selency. For example, I might find a plate, and not know where it comes from, but it might have a certain charm or a design that I've never seen before, and that's what makes it so interesting. I like a mix of pieces.

What is your favourite piece of furniture in your home?

I like my armchair designed by Geoffroy Harcourt – it's very comfortable and it has a seventies style, but goes with everything.

Can you share some of your advice for bargain-hunting?

- You have to accept that it takes time. And you need to take the time, too, to find out what you like. Look at other interiors for inspiration.
- Don't be afraid to buy vintage things – even if you change your mind after buying it, you can always resell it. The advantage of vintage and second-hand pieces is that they don't lose their value (unlike new items). This is very reassuring, and it's also why I change my interiors a lot. This way, I discover more pieces and products – and, of course, my taste evolves with the time.
- You need to define your criteria – your style, budget and

need. You need to marry style with function, too. Start with the function of a piece, and then think about the decorative and aesthetic aspects.

What are your favourite places in Paris?

My favourite restaurants include L'Hôtel Particulier, Le Bon Georges, Higuma, Brasserie Bellanger and Lucien la Chance. For shopping, I like Le Marché Saint Pierre, Les Puces de Saint Ouen, Merci and Mamiche (*boulangerie*). For places of interest, my favourites are Montmartre, la Rue Lepic, Les Abbesses and Île de la cité.

❖

ADDRESS BOOK

Concept stores & Parisian interiors brands
Beldy *(www.beldy.fr*
 – 32 Rue de Turbigo, 75003)
Caravane *(www.caravane.fr*
 – multiple locations)
Inès de La Fressange Paris *(www.inesdelafressange.fr*
 – 24 Rue de Grenelle, 75007)
Kann Design *(www.kanndesign.com*
 – 51 Rue des Vinaigriers, 75010)
La Trésorerie *(www.latresorerie.fr*
 – 11 & 8 Rue du Château d'Eau, 75010)
Maison Omani *(www.maisonomani.com*
 – 62 Boulevard de Ménilmontant, 75020)
Maison Sarah Lavoine – *(www.maisonsarahlavoine.com*
 – multiple locations)
Marin Montagut *(www.marinmontagut.com*
 – 48 Rue Madame, 75006)
Merci *(www.merci.com*
 – 111 Boulevard Beaumarchais, 75003)
The Socialite Family *(www.shop.thesocialitefamily.com*
 – 12 Rue Saint-Fiacre, 75002)

Bookshops & stationery
OFR Bookshop *(20 Rue Dupetit-Thouars, 75003)*
Papier Tigre *(www.papiertigre.fr*
 – 5 Rue des Calvaire, 75003)

Interiors & home life

Shakespeare and Company *(shakespeareandcompany.com
— 37 Rue de la Bûcherie, 75005)*
Yvon Lambert Bookshop *(www.shop.yvon-lambert.fr
— 14 Rue des Calvaire, 75003)*

Ceramics, glassware and home accessories
Affinité Terre *(www.affinite-terre.fr
— 13 Rue des Récollets, 75010)*
Astier de Villatte *(www.astierdevillatte.com)*
Atelier Vime *(www.ateliervime.com)*
Buly *(www.buly1803.com
— 6 Rue Bonaparte, 75006)*
Cire Trudon *(trudon.com
— 18 Rue de Seine, 75006)*
Deyrolle *(www.deyrolle.com
— 36 Rue du Bac, 75007)*
Diptyque *(www.diptyque.fr
— multiple locations)*
Empreintes *(www.empreintes-paris.com)*
Jamini *(www.jaminidesign.com
— 10 Rue du Château d'Eau, 75010)*
NOUS *(nousparis.com
— 19 Rue Clauzel, 75009)*
Racines Studio *(www.studioracines.com)*
Soufflerie *(www.lasoufflerie.com
— 26 Rue Lecourbe, 75015)*

Vintage & antiques
Les Puces de Saint Ouen *(Marché Paul Bert,
18 rue Paul Bert, 93400 Saint-Ouen)*

Chez Will *(55 Rue Damrémont, 75018)*
Galerie Patrick Seguin *(www.patrickseguin.com*
   – 5 Rue des Taillandiers, 75011)
L'Objet Qui Parle *(86 Rue des Martyrs, 75018)*
Selency *(www.selency.com)*

Dining out, drinking & café life

Parisian culinary culture

*'If you are lucky enough to have lived in Paris
as a young man, then wherever you go for the
rest of your life, it stays with you, for all of
Paris is a moveable feast'*
Ernest Hemingway

This chapter wasn't in my original book proposal, but
the more I wrote, and the further I delved into *la vie
Parisienne*, the more I realised that I could not talk about
practising Parisienne without mentioning a few of its main
ingredients. Dining out, *apéros*, catching up with a friend
in a café over a coffee and drinking good wine all inform

Parisian life. They are crucial elements in our everyday existence, and I would go so far as to say that my life, and the lives of many of my friends and colleagues, revolve around these activities. This is perhaps not so surprising, considering we live in a capital city, but, as with the other sections in this book, there is also something about the way Parisians regard food and drink that is a little different and – in my biased opinion – better. Their pursuit of pleasure and their *joie de vivre* certainly add colour to the way they approach their culinary culture.

When discussing the closure of restaurants for the second time last year due to the coronavirus pandemic, my Parisian friend Marie (who shared her skincare routine on page 112) exclaimed: 'But eating out and restaurants are life!' Although they are, at heart, homebodies, Parisians love nothing more than whiling away an evening with friends in a favourite brasserie or *cave à manger*. Parisians are fiercely loyal to their local restaurants, *caves à manger*, brasseries and cafés, to the extent that these places almost become second homes. Plus, Parisians are very social creatures and, especially in the summer, often prefer dining out to eating in. In fact, the foundations of many of my friendships have been built on a love of great food and wine, with some of my friends being chefs, food writers and food photographers. For them, the quest for good food (and drink) was the reason they moved to Paris. I have one friendship group in particular that's made up of mainly Americans who have been living in Paris for a number of years. We all became friends after meeting at a mutual friend's wedding in the autumn of 2019, forming a bond because we shared a love of cooking, eating and drinking. I certainly agree with Julia Child's adage 'People who love to eat are always the best people'. We took two group holidays together last year. This first was in July after the first *confinement* (France's name for lockdown): we rented a beautiful villa in the region of the Vars in the south of France. The second was a weekend staying in the grounds of Château de Courances, located an hour south of Paris, to celebrate a birthday. Our main activities on both trips were cooking and eating good food and drinking great wine (one friend, a chef, even had a couple of cases of natural wine sent to the address). We even had recipe spreadsheets, and conversations got a little fiery when ingredients were forgotten.

I've also had several heated debates with my Parisian boyfriend about food culture, local cuisine and cooking. He doesn't work in the food industry, nor does he consider himself particularly passionate about food: he just knows about where his food comes from, or at least has opinions about it (as most Parisians do). I like to think this is because food is so integral to his culture and Parisian upbringing. We have, for example, discussed the myriad different types of cheeses used for specific recipes, such as tartiflette, fondue and raclette; the merits of farm-produced products and how to recognise them by their labels; where to buy the best *foie gras*; which is the better cut of pork for lardons (*poitrine* – pork belly); and which type of vinegar is best to use in a vinaigrette (red wine). Thanks to him, I discovered a very special type of chicken – *poularde de Bresse* – which has *appellation d'origine contrôlée* status, meaning it can only be produced in Bresse, a historic region in the east of France, near Lyon. The chickens (only white) have to be raised according to certain regulations, with a minimum of 10 square metres in which to roam freely. Once dubbed 'the queen of poultry, the poultry of kings' by esteemed French lawyer, politician and gourmand Jean Anthelme Brillat-Savarin (1755–1826), it is the chicken that many French Parisian families will eat for Christmas, and the very same that I ate at my boyfriend's mother's house during my first Christmas in Paris. On our first weekend away together, I followed him through the aisles in the supermarket like a small child, fascinated by the products that he was selecting for our weekend cooking: *farcie* meat (stuffing) for stuffed tomatoes and courgettes, which comes ready-minced with herbs and onions; farm-produced yogurt; and Reblochon cheese – the only cheese you can make a real tartiflette with. I was in awe – if not a little intimidated by his seemingly intuitive food knowledge. In previous relationships, I had always been the one who was most into food and cooking, so this was a new experience for me.

When we first starting dating, he refused to go to certain establishments. Some were ones that I rather enjoyed, for their French-ness (or so I thought). According to him, though, they were too touristy, not actually very French and didn't use quality products. I also noticed an immediate and stark contrast in the way that we each cooked. He favours very simple food, such as omelettes, *magret de canard* (duck breast) and green salads. My cooking habits (although they have become more 'Parisian' in that I try to take more heed of seasonal and local produce) are still rather rich in sauces and exotic ingredients from faraway countries, such as Mexico, India and Thailand. I think this comes from having grown up in the UK, a country that's admittedly never been particularly celebrated for its own culinary heritage, but is very good at embracing international cuisine (something I do miss about living in London).

Good food, good drink and, in many ways, coffee (or at least its cafés), are key elements in a Parisian's daily lifestyle and a big part of what it means to be Parisian. The city's culinary culture is one of the main reasons (as well as her beautiful architecture) that so many foreigners flock to Paris each year to visit and live. This important relationship with, and rich history of, food and drink is also why budding chefs make a beeline here to study. Paris's culinary history is long and colourful, and the city has some of the best cooking schools in the world, Le Cordon Bleu being just one example. It's also why the likes of Rachel Khoo's *The Little Paris Kitchen* book and TV series were such hits in the UK – because there is such an appetite for cooking and eating in a more Parisian fashion. In the same way, once Julia Child translated and broke down French cooking into manageable, bite-sized pieces, Americans began devouring French food, sparking a new-found obsession with Paris.

It is worth mentioning that, although the city is rich in culinary culture and heritage, it has taken Paris a little longer to embrace new trends – which is also true in some of the other areas that I discuss in this book. Food fashions that are already rife in places like New York and London tend not to hit Paris until much later. It's an aspect of Parisian living that expats and Parisians who have spent time abroad sometimes find frustrating, although I would argue that having a slower-paced lifestyle is no bad thing. It's undeniable, too, that its strong ties and loyalty to its past is part of what makes Paris so charming, and why good restaurants in the French capital tend to last longer. This opinion is reiterated by Parisian-born TV presenter Philippine Darblay, who spent six years living in London in her early twenties, and who I interview later in this section (page 272): 'Sometimes I want Paris to be shaken a bit more. It's like a small village, and they are not always interested in things that aren't French.' But, she goes on to say, the big plus in Paris is that restaurants have longevity – they will last at least ten years and maintain their popularity. It's also important to note that this slight resistance to change has given foreigners and expats like myself opportunities to innovate. One example is The Kale Project, launched by New Yorker Kristen Beddard, who relocated to Paris with her husband. She couldn't find kale anywhere in Paris. It was a vegetable that had been integral to her cooking back home in New

York, so she decided to make it her mission to encourage farmers to produce it and markets to sell it. She published a book about her experience, *Bonjour Kale*, in 2016.

Despite its slowness to change, the culinary landscape has transformed since I moved to Paris eight years ago. Amateur chefs first arriving in the city to learn the art of French cuisine have gone on to open their own eateries inspired by their heritage, while experienced foreign chefs who brought their existing knowledge and *savoir-faire* have put their own stamp on the city.

Besides an appreciation for good food and drink, and an understanding of where it comes from, I've also found that the Parisians have a unique relationship with eating and drinking. This, of course, ties in to how they approach beauty, wellbeing, exercise and, well, their over-all lifestyle: it is more 'curated'. While I don't subscribe to the cliché bolstered by the 2004 book *French Women Don't Get Fat* (although I admit I never hear my French friends telling me they need to go on a diet), I do think there is something in the way that the Parisians view food that is healthier and more balanced than many other cultures. They make sure to buy fresh, seasonal produce, and consume it in more moderate quantities. As Monica de La Villardière pointed out when I interviewed her on page 82: 'They indulge with a certain amount of restraint, which is also how I would define the way that French women eat. For example, here bingeing is a no-no.'

It's also worth pointing out that I did, in fact, shed some excess weight when I first moved to Paris – and not intentionally. Of course, everyone's experience is different, but I had a rather poor diet back in the UK, fuelled by crisps, cakes, sweets and a little too much alcohol, and I rarely made the time to eat properly. When I moved to France, I immediately stopped snacking. This was perhaps because I was no longer working in an office with an overflowing 'snacks' table, partly because moving to Paris made me slow down, as the pace of life is just that bit slower here, but also certainly because the snacks that I was so used to – and, admittedly, addicted to – just weren't available. There were no salt and vinegar Squares, Skittles, Galaxy Minstrels, prawn cocktail Skips or heavy sponge cakes. My food shopping habits also changed. Here, within each *quartier*, the main street is lined with a small town's worth of local establishments, like *boulangeries*, *poissonnèrie* (fishmongers) and *épiciers* (grocers), along with the weekly markets that pop up two to three times a week. I was fuelling my body with healthier food. Of course, some habits die hard, and I do still indulge in salt and vinegar crisps every now again (much to the dismay of my Parisian boyfriend, who looks at me in shock as I devour a big bag in one sitting), but ultimately I have learned to look at food and alcohol very differently. As well as snacking less, I just don't overindulge like I used to. So much of my approach to food now is about balance and moderation. Because of this, I also stopped worrying about what I ate, and I no longer count calories (I used to have an app that counted them for me when I lived in London). But enough about calories and weight loss, and on to the good stuff – the Parisian approach to food and drink.

And so in this section, I'm going to reveal how to perfect the Parisian *apéro*, share some of my favourite wines and champagne, and talk about *caves à manger*, my places *préférées* to drink and dine in Paris. I'll present the food-and-drink-based wisdom of a few of my friends, as well as people I admire working in the food and wine industry (both French and expat), such as food photographer Joann Pai, presenter Philippine Darblay, baker Frank Barron, city-guide writer Yasmin Zeinab, café owner Fanny Flory, and writer and author Rebekah Peppler. I will also share the parts of Parisian culinary life that I find the most interesting and integral to my experience of living here, in the hope that they will inspire your next meal, glass of wine or restaurant trip, as well as helping you navigate Paris's food and bar scene on your next visit.

Drinking: an education in good wine

'Wine makes every meal an occasion, every table more elegant, every day more civilised'
André Simon

We English have a reputation in France. Yes, I'm afraid so. According to the French, we are known for drinking – *a lot*. And if what we are drinking is wine, it's usually not very good. When I was dating, I had dates with French men where, once the conversation turned to drink, they would raise their eyebrows, a smirk would spread across their mouths, and they would say, 'Ah yes, but you are English. You like to drink.' This would be followed by my justification and explanation that no, I am in fact a lightweight – *a petite joueuse*. I can't actually tolerate much alcohol – perhaps, I would say, I am therefore not very English? (I am only half English, after all). To which they'd usually reply that they didn't believe me, and could they offer me another glass of wine? I have even had to defend myself to my Parisian friends on various occasions, when the conversation jokingly turns to me and my English ways. But who can blame them, when England is so widely known for its binge-drinking culture?

It's no secret that France is famous for its wine (and champagne) production, and perhaps that's why the French have a little more respect for it: because they know exactly where it comes from, how it's made and just how much work goes into a good bottle of wine. When I first moved to France, I was a self-professed philistine when it came to wine and champagne. I knew what I liked and didn't like when I tasted it, but I was rather lost when it came to choosing wine from a menu or from the supermarket shelves. My memories of wine in my twenties were of bad Sauvignon Blanc and Pinot Grigio, and of mixing red wine with Coke in Spain (yes, that's legitimately a drink there, known as *calimocho* or *kalimotxo*). Alcohol was (I'm a little embarrassed to reveal) mainly for getting drunk, not for enjoying with food or over good conversation. This was in stark contrast to the attitude of my French friends, many of who seemed to have come out of the womb armed with an encyclopaedic knowledge of wine. So living in Paris has, for me, also been an education in good food and wine – as it has in so many other areas of my life.

Wine and champagne are a huge part of a Parisian's heritage. They live in the second-largest wine-producing country in the world, and so they grew up with it: it was on the table during dinner when they were children, and they were usually allowed to try it, in small amounts. Many of my French friends have told me that this was just part of growing up, and so drinking alcohol as adolescents wasn't a taboo. I have never heard stories of my French friends bingeing on alcohol, nor have I seen examples of it in the streets. It's deemed decidedly 'un-Parisian' and the opposite of being chic and elegant to get drunk at a party or event, as demonstrated by the instruction in *How to be Parisian* to: 'Sip your champagne, but never get too drunk.'

As I quickly discovered, if you live in Paris, you need to know a bit about wine. It's a sign of being cultured, of being Parisian and French. If you develop this knowledge as a foreigner, it also shows you've made an effort to live here and embrace the culture. You need to know what wine to choose in a restaurant, and what kind to bring to a party. I now believe being able to choose a good bottle of wine is an important life skill. I was fortunate enough to work for Bordeaux Wines for two years, the brand that represents the 700-plus châteaux in the South West region of France. I looked after their social media and marketing strategy for the UK market. During my time with the brand, I was lucky enough to visit Bordeaux and its historic châteaux on various occasions. I learned about *appellations*, *cépages* (grape varieties), and how to taste wine. And inspired by my initial wine lessons with Bordeaux Wines, I have learned over the years more about *accord mets et vins* (wine and food pairings), so I now know that oysters taste great with Muscadet and Sancerre; Pouilly-Fumé pairs well with goat's cheese;

Côtes de Rhône is a good go-to red when you need to bring a bottle to a party or dinner; and Sauternes is a delicious dessert wine, to be enjoyed on special occasions and when there is something sweet to indulge in.

French wine to know & buy

'Forget sport, embroidery, gardening and even cooking; for a Parisienne, the most important skill to have is the ability to choose wine. Wine is a way of life in Paris'

Lauren Bastide, *In Paris*

As you've gathered by now, I love a good glass of wine, and I totally subscribe to Lauren Bastide's statement above that wine is a way of life in Paris. I look forward to drinking wine with dinner or on the weekend with friends at an *apéro*, and I always have a good bottle at home just in case. I also enjoy browsing the wine sections in the *supermarchés* or at a local *cave*. Equally, I love opening a wine menu in a restaurant, or reading the names of wines chalked up on a board above the bar. I also have a habit of asking a waiter or whoever is serving the wine at a work event to let me have a look at the bottle's label, often taking a photo of it for my Vivino wine app, so I can come back to it later.

While I love wines from other countries, namely Cloudy Bay Sauvignon Blanc from New Zealand and Portuguese wine, especially vinho verde (green wine) and reds from the Douro region, I'll reserve my words here for French wine. So, here are a few of my favourites. Hopefully this will give you a little crash course in French wines, so that when you're next in the supermarket or dining in a French restaurant, the task of choosing a good bottle will be that little bit easier.

❧

Wine glossary

Before we dive in, here are a few key words and phrases to help you with your wine knowledge.

French

appellation **or AOC** – the legally defined and protected geographical indication used to identify where grapes are grown for a specific type of wine

cépages – grape varieties

assemblage – when two grape varieties are blended together

savoir-faire – know-how

terroir – literally meaning 'land', in this case it's the combination of soil, climate and other factors that influence the character of the wine

un vin doux – a sweet wine

un vin sec – a dry wine

un bouchon – a cork

un tire-bouchon – a corkscrew

bouchonné – corked

je suis pompette – I am tipsy

je suis bourré – I am drunk (slang)

English

legs – the term used to describe the wine drops that
look like they're crawling down the side of the
glass after swirling. Many believe the more legs,
the better, as it denotes a better-quality wine, but
it only really illustrates that the liquid contains
alcohol – the more alcohol content, the more 'legs'.

nose – the wine's aromas

tannins – found in grape skins, they help give
structure to wine

maceration – the process of skins and grape juices
combining together

Useful descriptive words: complex, full-bodied,
supple (smooth), dry, sweet, structured, bold,
intense, rich, light, fresh, buttery, oily

Popular aroma descriptions: toasted bread,
butter, oak, red fruits, zest, candied fruit, leather,
peach, pepper, vanilla, caramel, chocolate, coffee,
grapefruit, liquorice

❖

My favourite French white wines

Pouilly-Fumé – My current go-to every day wine, Pouilly-
Fumé is a dry white produced from the Sauvignon Blanc
grape in the Loire Valley, in the centre of France. It's
called *fumé*, meaning 'smoky', because when the grapes

reach maturity, they look a little grey in colour and they have a slightly 'smoky' aroma due to their terroir. Pouilly-Fumé tastes great with *apèro* foods in summer, such as creamy cheeses and salads and with heavier dishes in winter like *moules marinière*. It is one of my favourite wines to enjoy with oysters, which are in season from September to April.

Sancerre – Sancerre is my other favourite French Sauvignon Blanc wine. It is also produced in the Loire region, but on the river's left bank, the opposite side to Pouilly-Fumé. It is probably the best-known *appellation* of French Sauvignon Blanc both in and outside of France. Sancerre wines are dry and aromatic, and my preferred choice for an *apéro* in summer as they have a tendency to be zesty, light and refreshing. The vines are grown in soils comprised of chalky limestone and clay, making them on the whole less complex than Pouilly-Fumé, whose grapes are grown in richer soils of clay-flint. This is my favourite wine to pair with prawns and white fish in warmer weather.

Pouilly-Fuissé – Funnily enough, as I mentioned on page 5, I have a photograph of me as a child standing under a sign of Pouilly-Fuissé during a family holiday in France. Who knew that twenty-four years later, I would move to Paris and this wine would become one of my favourites? You'd be forgiven for confusing Fuissé with Fumé, which I have on a few occasions, but Pouilly-Fuissé is made from 100 per cent Chardonnay grapes and hails from the Mâconnais region of Burgundy, in the central-east area of France near Dijon. Vineyards, crossing the boundaries of four villages – Chantre, Fuissé, Solutré-Pouilly and Vergisson – are built into rocky terrain dating back 200 million years, where one of the most evolved prehistoric cultures once thrived. These wines are, on the whole, more expensive than Pouilly-Fumé as they are richer and more structured. They are also a slighter darker yellow in colour, and have more legs when you swirl them. I wouldn't drink a Pouilly-Fuissé for an *apéro*: they should be reserved for a sit-down main meal.

Chablis & Petit Chablis – I'm grouping these two wines together, as the only difference between them is the soil in which the grapes are grown, and that Petit Chablis is lighter and more refreshing. It is not a lesser wine, so to speak. They too are both produced from the Chardonnay grape, but in the north west of the Burgundy region. When compared to the Sauvignon Blancs (such as Sancerre and Pouilly-Fumé), Chablis is generally a little fuller-bodied and more complex on the palette (in my opinion). Although they are still lighter than another famous Burgundy style, Côte de Beaune, which is produced on the other side of the region. I tend to drink these wines with anything from fish to dishes that come with creamy sauces and even sometimes with Thai and Indian curries (although a sweet wine is generally a better pairing, to help balance out the heat.) They are also the wines I order in a bar if I want just one good glass, as I tend to savour them for longer.

My go-to red wines

Côtes du Rhône – Côtes du Rhône is a classic, easy-to-drink red wine, and certainly one of France's most popular and well-known *appellations*. I'm sure this is due, at least in part, to the fact that it has been produced in the region since before Roman times and was a favourite of royalty before they (literally) lost their heads. The vineyards spread throughout the Rhône Valley in the south of France near Avignon, and the reds are produced predominantly from Grenache or Syrah grapes. This is the red wine that I buy to bring to dinners and *apéros* in autumn and winter, because it's around the middle price range and isn't too heavy: it's the safe option when you don't know what to buy.

Bordeaux – I have a soft spot for this region of winemaking, not only because it is beautiful (I could happily live in the city of Bordeaux, which is like a smaller, warmer version of Paris), but also because it's the region of France I have visited the most often. This is France's largest and most famous winemaking region, encompassing more than 700 châteaux surrounding the Garonne River, so I'm thinking you've probably heard of it. If you don't know what to choose, go for a straightforward red Bordeaux or Médoc/Haut-Médoc. My personal favourite is a Pauillac, specifically from Château Pichon Baron de Longueville, but it's very pricey. A bottle goes for around 100€, so it's certainly not one I'd buy for a casual dinner.

The Graves region of Bordeaux, on the left bank of the Garonne river also produces the most delicious dessert wines that I have ever tasted – most famously Sauternes. This syrupy, honey-coloured wine is mainly enjoyed with desserts on special occasions, like Christmas, when you have time to spend the whole day drinking and eating.

Gigondas – I like to think of Gigondas as my trump card, and the one I pull out when I want to show that I know a little more about wine. It's a lesser-known wine *appellation*, as it produces much smaller quantities than some of France's bigger players, but it's by far one of my favourites, so I wanted to include it. This winemaking region and eponymous village is located in the Vaucluse department, in the South of France, to the northeast of Avignon and within the Rhône Valley. I discovered it a few years ago, thanks to a visit to the village following a wedding. Needless to say, we left with a couple of boxes. These wines are heavy, bold and full of character, and have plenty of 'legs' thanks to their high alcohol content; they shouldn't be downed quickly during an *apéro*, but rather savoured during a long sit-down meal with friends and preferably in colder weather.

Champagne brands to know & buy

I should point out, in case you don't know, that true champagne can only be produced in the Champagne region of France, a forty-five-minute train ride northeast of Paris.

Ruinart – Ruinart is the oldest champagne house in France, and so the one I will mention first. It was founded in Reims in 1729 by Thomas Ruinart and was the first house to ship rosé champagne across Europe in 1764. Ruinart's uncle, Dom Thierry, learned about a new 'wine with bubbles' through his studies (he was a Benedictine monk and scholar), during which he was exposed to court life. He passed on this knowledge to Thomas, and the Ruinart champagne house was born. Today, Ruinart is still one of the most revered champagne brands in the business.

I was invited to the house last summer to discover their latest champagne brunch offering (a set menu on weekends) and was wowed by the jaw-dropping size of the cellars, which resemble the huge caves of the Lonely Mountain, where Smaug the dragon lay sleeping in *Lord of the Rings*. I was also impressed that, every year, they collaborate with a different artist. In 2020 it was the British artist David Shrigley, who created works for the house and squiggled on the floors and walls of the cellars. Just to visit the *maison* is an experience in itself. For my first Christmas in Paris, we drank Ruinart Rosé, and then had Ruinart Brut for New Year's Eve.

Möet & Chandon – This was the first champagne that I ever tasted in the UK. I remember thinking how fancy it was to buy a bottle of champagne for New Year's Eve, or to celebrate a friend's birthday. Möet & Chandon is one of the largest champagne houses, and was founded in 1743 by Claude Möet. Incidentally, for those of you who are fans of *The Crown*, Möet & Chandon hold a Royal Warrant to supply champagne to Queen Elizabeth II. This may go some way towards explaining why this was the first champagne that I learned about growing up in the UK.

Perrier-Jouët – Perrier-Jouët was established in 1811 by Pierre Nicolas Perrier and Rose Adelaide Jouët, and boasts one of the most beautifully designed logos that I've ever seen. It incorporates an anemone flower created by the master of Art Nouveau, Emile Galle, inspired by the founders' affinity for nature. The champagne is created from the Chardonnay grape, which was a bold decision at the time and helped to establish the house as one of the best in the world. I was lucky enough to attend a Dîner en Blanc with the brand in the grounds of Les Invalides. It's a huge outdoor dinner organised every year in Paris (they now host it in other countries too). Guests have to wear white and bring their own food, tables and chairs!

How to create the perfect Parisian apéro

The '*apéro*' (otherwise known as my favourite time of day) is a French institution that basically means a drink and a small bite to eat before dinner, say around 7 p.m. *Apéro* derives from the word 'aperitif', which comes from the Latin *aperire*, meaning 'to open'. Historically, one took an aperitif (an alcoholic drink) before dinner to help 'open' the appetite. Today, it's an occasion to meet friends, or to round off the working day with a leisurely drink.

I fervently look forward to *apéro* time, as it signifies a moment to relax (especially if you enjoy it after work during the week). It's the perfect opportunity to take pleasure in a good glass of wine, and to snack on anything from a chunk of cheese with bread to oysters with a fresh squeeze of lemon and a teaspoon of Mignonette (the classic shallot vinaigrette). If it's a special occasion, like Christmas or New Year, you might even have *foie gras*.

Apéro is the only time of day when Parisians actually 'snack', but in my experience, when it comes to socialising with my French friends, the *apéro* can also become a sort of lazy Parisian dinner. It's just as delicious as having a main meal, and can be just as filling – as long as you can get your hands on enough bread. In fact, if you're invited to an *apéro*, the polite thing to do is to take your own bread, along with a piece of cheese (preferably purchased from a *fromagerie*) and a nice bottle of wine. A good host will usually provide these things, but it's best to arrive prepared, and in Paris it's usually expected that everyone will contribute. I've been to numerous soirées where the *apéro* has turned into dinner and there hasn't always been enough food to eat, so I now always pre-empt this by bringing extra supplies so I don't go hungry or get drunk due to drinking wine on an empty stomach. As with most cities that lie on the southern side of Europe, Paris is pretty relaxed when it comes to dinnertime, which can be anything from 8–10 p.m.

Creating your own *apéro*

As it is such a staple of Parisian life, I couldn't write a chapter on food and drink without explaining everything you need to create your very own *apéro* for all seasons. Of course there's a wealth of different items and nibbles that you can serve for *apéro* depending on your taste, but the following items are for me, the main ingredients.

A good bottle of wine – A Sauvignon Blanc, such as Pouilly-Fumé or Sancerre, in spring and summer, and generally a red in winter, such as a Côtes de Rhône or Haut-Médoc. I also like to drink rosé, such as a Côtes de Provence, on particularly warm days in the height of summer.

Oysters (April to September) – Preferably 3–6 per person, with a squeeze of fresh lemon and Mignonette sauce, which you can make yourself by finely dicing half a shallot and adding it to half a ramekin of red wine vinegar. I always add a splash of whatever white wine I'm drinking for good measure. Pair oysters with white wines.

Cheeses – If it's summer and you're drinking white or rosé, the majority of your cheese selection should be creamy goat's cheeses and blue cheeses such as Roquefort. In winter, go for harder cheeses, such as Comté or Comtel (they have a tendency to sweat in the summer heat, so I usually save them for cooler weather). Another winter favourite is to pop a Camembert in the oven and, once gooey, drizzle with honey and finish with a sprig of rosemary. You and your guests can dip ripped off pieces of baguette directly into the cheese.

Charcuterie (cured meats – the name comes from the French word *chair* meaning 'flesh' and *cuit*, which means 'cooked') – *Saucisson sec* is a must – ideally with minimal fat. One of my favourites, if you can find it, is Saint Agaune, which has less fat than most. Another popular charcuterie addition is *jambon bayonne*, which is a cured ham hailing from the town of Bayonne in south west France.

Bread – Try to get your hands on a *tradition* – this is a baguette made from wholewheat and baked on the day of sale.

Olives – Generally green, although black olive tapenade is also good addition to your *apéro* spread.

Dips – Hummus is an obvious choice, but you can also add tzatziki and taramasalata – I'm not really a fan (although I love most kinds of fish), but have noticed that most of my Parisian French friends are, and it was the *apéro* that my boyfriend's mum served before dinner on Christmas Eve. With a squeeze of fresh lemon, I found myself reaching for more than usual, plus it paired very well with the champagne rosé that I'd brought with me.

Nuts – Almonds, pistachios and cashews are the best options.

Grapes – Not only do these look pretty on the table, but they will also offer a refreshing break from the richer flavours present.

Tableware – You don't need much: a nice set of wine glasses (or deliberately mismatched vintage ones); a linen tablecloth and serviettes, a few sharp knives to cut the cheeses, a good bottle opener; small plates, so your guests don't get crumbs all over your cream rug; candles for decoration; and, of course, the guests.

Rebekah Peppler's Kir cocktail

American expat Rebekah (@rebekahpeppler) is the author of James Beard-nominated book *Aperitif: Cocktail Hour the French Way* and *À Table: Recipes For Cooking + Eating the French Way*. She knows how to make a mean cocktail, so I asked her for one of her favourites, which could easily accompany an *apéro*.

This is the drink I make when I'm trying to recreate the experience of drinking with friends at Le Cristal Bar, a treasure of a corner bar in the 10th arrondissement. If I'm going for the *vrai expérience* Cristal, I pour a bit heavy on the cassis, make sure there's a basket of slightly stale, slightly broken, often-refilled potato chips nearby, and – perhaps most importantly – I drink one too many. If I'm in the mood for something bubbly, I swap in sparkling white or rosé wine for the still white, turning it into a Kir Royale.

Serves 1

½–1 tablespoon (7.5–15ml) crème de cassis
125–175ml dry white wine, such as Aligoté, or sparkling white
    or rosé wine, chilled

Pour the crème de cassis into a wine glass. Top with wine and serve immediately.

❧

My boyfriend's vinaigrette dressing

Despite growing up on a healthy diet, when it came to condiments and sauces, these were always shop-bought. My American mum loves nothing more than to smother her salads with a calorific Caesar dressing or ranch sauce. They're the flavours she grew up with in the US, and the ones I was accustomed to until I moved to Paris and realised the error of my ways. Soon, like the Parisians, I started making my own dressings from olive oil and vinegar. While I usually made mine with balsamic vinegar, I have since learned the art of a good French vinaigrette thanks to my Parisian boyfriend.

All you need to do is toss it with green salad, preferably fresh 'leaf' lettuce, or iceberg if you like a bit more crunch. It goes with everything from an omelette to pasta or *magret de canard* and sautéed potatoes, which is exactly what we ate for New Year's Eve 2020.

Makes 2 servings
1 tablespoon red wine vinegar
2 tablespoons olive oil (you can adjust
    the amount a little depending on how
    strong you like your vinaigrette to be)
½ teaspoon Dijon mustard
¼ teaspoon mustard à *l'Ancienne*
    (or wholegrain mustard)

Pinch of salt and a twist of ground black pepper
Simply add all the ingredients to a large salad bowl, and
whisk together with a fork. Add pre-washed lettuce to
the bowl, toss together and *voilà* – that's it.

A chat about Parisian food culture with Philippine Darblay

Philippine (@philoudarblay) is a TV presenter and all-round food aficionado. She presents the show *Très Très Bon* on Paris Première, which scouts new food places in Paris and France, as well as appearing on their culture show, *J'ai un Ticket*. She is also the community builder for Soho House Paris. She grew up in the 5th arrondissement and spent six years in London, where she also studied for a postgraduate degree in food as an art form at Central Saint Martin's.

Why did you want to work within the food industry?
I always thought there was a connection between art and food and wanted to explore that. Chefs are designers as much as fashion designers are. They use different means, ingredients instead of fabric, but it's the same process. They have a vision and they create.

Who or what inspired you to work in the culinary world?
I would say that the role models I grew up with were key: my grandmother, who was from Brittany, and my dad, who cooks incredibly well and brought back recipes from Italy and Scotland. I was also inspired by a lady from the village in Austria where I spent all my summers. They all opened my eyes to the topic in different ways. Travel helped to shape this passion, too: London, for the incredible diversity of options; Copenhagen, for its very local and innovative food culture;

the rest of France, for its traditions... any country I visited, really. Food even became the core reason for my travels, and I've met so many friends this way, too.

Why did you come back to Paris?

I left France from the ages of 19 to 26, but I wanted to rethink the way I was working, so I returned. London life can get a bit crazy, and I was running everywhere. Paris is sometimes too slow, but the Parisians are very good at taking the time for themselves, so I came back.

What do you love most about Parisian culinary culture?

It's no news that Paris is not the most innovative city, but one big quality that Parisian restaurants have is that they last for a long time. Not just the old-school restaurants that have been around for 100 years: even new places tend to last for at least ten years. For example, my favourite restaurant, Clamato, has been around for a decade now.

What are your favourite places to eat and drink in Paris?

For dining: Clamato, CAM, Chez Georges.

For drinking: Bambino, Serpent à Plumes for the interiors and Caves Legrand for their wine list.

Philippine's recipe for courgette and goat's cheese quiche

Serves 6

4 small, firm courgettes

olive oil, for frying

1 garlic clove, chopped

a handful of fresh herbs of your choice (such as basil, parsley
  or chives)
100g pine nuts
375g homemade or ready-rolled shortcrust pastry
100g goat's cheese
4 eggs
2 tablespoons double cream
salt and freshly ground black pepper

Preheat the oven to 190°C/170°C fan/375°F/gas mark 5.

Peel the courgettes in strips, leaving a strip of green skin between
every part that you peel, then slice into rounds.

Heat some olive oil in a non-stick pan over a medium heat and add
the courgette slices. Season with salt and pepper, and then cook for
10–15 minutes until cooked but still firm, stirring regularly.

Add the garlic and herbs (unless you're using basil, which you don't
want to cook). Stir to combine, then transfer to a colander to let
any juices drain.

In a separate dry frying pan, toast the pine nuts over a medium heat
for 2–3 minutes or until golden brown.

In a bowl, whisk together the eggs and cream with a fork. Season
with salt and pepper, and if you're using basil, stir it in.

Roll out the dough and use it to line the base and sides of a non-
stick, loose-bottomed 23cm baking tin. (You can also line the tin
with baking paper to prevent the pastry from sticking.) Use a fork to
prick small holes in it, then blind-bake for 10 minutes.

Remove the partly baked pastry case from the oven and arrange the courgette slices on the bottom. Layer on the goat's cheese slices, on top, then the toasted pine nuts, and finally pour over the egg mixture.

Bake for about 20–25 minutes and serve with a green salad

Caves à manger

'Wine is inspiring and adds greatly to the joy of living'
Napoleon Bonaparte

While I love dining in a beautiful restaurant with attentive table service and clearly defined starters, mains and desserts, my favourite places to eat in Paris are undoubtedly *caves à manger*. These are wine bars where you can also eat in (but are not necessarily obliged to.) They are usually small (some tiny) establishments specialising in wines, consisting mainly of a bar, with a few stools, a limited number of tables and often a wall stocked from floor to ceiling with wine bottles.

They're intimate and cosy, and the wines come with a highly curated selection of small accompanying plates, which can easily replace dinner, depending on how hungry you are. For me, they encapsulate everything that I love about Paris's dining scene and what makes it so special. They're fun and exciting,

and I love the casual dining style, the noise, the buzz of conversation, the proximity to your neighbour as you try not to knock over their glass of wine, the closeness you often have to the kitchen if you sit at the bar, which also might entail chats with the barman or owner (and the people next to you.) It's a dining experience that I haven't had anywhere else. They're also the best spots for solo dining. And because they often have later closing times, these spaces sometimes turn into parties as the music gets turned up. They are the best places to visit if you want to experience the true colours of the city's culinary scene. They are what help make Paris Paris. So, here are a few of my favourites.

Yard Cave – I was a little late to the party when I finally visited Yard Cave for the first time after moving to the 11th arrondissement and finding myself within walking distance of this charcoal-fronted bar, which stands next to the restaurant of the same name – but it was certainly worth the wait. You have to get there early to find a free stool at the L-shaped bar, but if you can grab a spot, you're likely to remain there all evening, ordering small plates and glasses of wine from the tall, glass-fronted cupboards stacked with bottles.

La Buvette – Not to be confused with the equally cosy restaurant in the 9th arrondissement, La Buvette serves up natural wines and small accompanying plates of cheese and charcuterie. The tiny spot is a former dairy that has been decked out with a large marble-topped wooden bar, terrazzo-tile flooring and a few small tables. What it lacks in space it makes up for in atmosphere, and customers and locals will often spill out on to the pavement on warm summer nights.

Bar Martin – Boire et Manger – More restaurant than *cave*, thanks to its greater square footage and its fuller menu of beautifully presented small plates, this spot still boasts the same relaxed atmosphere of most *caves à manger*, making it the perfect prelude, and a great spot for a glass of wine before moving on to dinner at popular restaurants like Au Passage or Clown Bar if you're with a larger group of people.

Septime la Cave – Septime la Cave is the one I've visited most in Paris. It was my local while I lived in the 11th arrondissement, and admittedly my preferred meeting place for dates when I didn't want to travel across town. It's also the bar I go to when waiting for a table at Clamato (my favourite seafood restaurant), which is owned by the same team. But I've also spent the entire evening here. There's always a fun and lively atmosphere and with a reputation that reaches far beyond France's borders (it's been cited in places like the Cereal City Guides and CN Traveller), it has one of the city's most international crowds.

Paul Bert Cave – Although small, Rue Paul Bert is one of the 11th arrondissement's buzziest streets (not unlike a village itself) thanks to the fact that its packed full of great restaurants, a *boulangerie*, an *épicerie*, a ham shop and a trio of establishments – a *chocolaterie*, *pâtisserie* and brasserie – all owned by the famed *pâtisserie* chef Cyril Lynac. I lived on a street perpendicular to Rue Paul Bert for two years, and while I sampled all the restaurants lining its pavements, my favourite was the tiniest – this *cave à manger* – and I would often race to the bar during summer to grab the table outside before it became too busy.

A conversation about food & Paris's culinary culture with Joann Pai

Joann (@sliceofpai) is a Canadian expat who moved to Paris in 2015. She's a self-taught food and lifestyle photographer, regularly creating content for Paris-based restaurants and publications like *CN Traveler* and *The New York Times*. She's has six books under her belt (which she also photographed). She's married to a Parisian who she met by chance in a bar within three months of arriving in the French capital.

Why were you inspired to move to Paris?

Since my first visit to Paris, I've always felt a strong connection to this beautiful city and dreamed of spending more time here someday. When I left my nine-to-five job to pursue a career in photography, I took the chance and applied for a one-year visa. What attracted me to Paris was mostly the *'bon vivant'* attitude of the French. I romanced about the idea of sitting around the dinner table for hours, just talking and enjoying the food and wine. I love how passionate the French are when it comes to food, and their long history of food culture, which is something that I didn't have growing up in USA and Canada.

What do you love most about Parisian culinary culture?

I think that it's a very exciting time to be in Paris, as things are starting to change. For the longest time, the culinary scene here was like a museum. Tourists came mostly to experience classic French food. These days, you can see much more international influence in the culture, and foreigners contributing other interpretations of French food. In addition, there's much more emphasis on using fresh, seasonal ingredients.

What do you think is the most interesting thing about how the Parisians approach food and drink (both culture and consumption)?

In general, they're much more rigid about what to eat when. Breakfast, lunch, *goûter*, *apéro*, then entrée, *plat fromage*, dessert, *digestif*. As an anglophone, I feel like I can have breakfast for dinner, or snack all day.

What can we learn from the Parisians in terms of culinary culture and the way they approach eating, drinking and dining out?

I grew up in America, where bigger meant better. Whenever we dined out, we would always have leftovers. Here, the portions are generally smaller, and it's encouraged to simply order what you can consume.

What are your favourite places to eat and drink in Paris?

For dining: Mokonuts, Comice, Frenchie Wine Bar. For drinking: Septime la Cave, Bisou, Bar Martin.

Parisian markets

'It was here that Paris revealed herself to me first, teaching me the questions to ask to draw her story out, and allowing me to taste her character in what I thought were insignificant moments . . . The vitality of the market; the sounds of conversations and food stalls; the smells of fish, herbs, onions, roasting meats; bright végétal colours and deep earth still clinging to roots – all of these layered and piled on top of each other like books in an old Parisian bookstore'

Jackie Kai Ellis, *The Measure of my Powers*

Fresh food markets, like wine and *apéros* are very much a part of Paris's culinary DNA. They are not just places to mooch around in, pick up a bite to eat or sightsee (which is my experience of most markets in London and New York, for example) – they are part of daily life, and they are where many of the city's inhabitants will go to do their regular food shopping. However, if you do want to sightsee, explore, and experience a taste of real Parisian life, the city's food markets are a great place to do it. In Paris, markets are not just for chefs, food aficionados, tourists or decoration – yes they are alive and fizzing with energy, but they also serve up exceptionally good homegrown and locally reared produce, as well as exotic

itcms from afar. They're also the places that helped me change my unhealthy eating habits in favour of a more balanced diet.

When I lived in the 10th arrondissement, I would visit the market almost every Sunday to purchase fish, cheese, fruit, vegetables and flowers. It became my Sunday afternoon ritual. I have never been one to enjoy Sundays, and have often suffered from bouts of the 'Sunday scaries', but going to the market every week made me look forward to Sundays for the first time in my life. There's something special about a French market, particularly in the capital. They are full of sights, sounds and especially smells: the sour tang of cheese from the *fromagerie* stand that can make your eyes water; the sizzling scents from roasting chicken wafting up in puffs of smoke; the fresh aroma of fish and seafood that suddenly transports you to the sea, conjuring up memories of being a child wrapped up in a coat and scarf, stomping your wellied foot into soggy seaweed at low tide. The harried calls from the fruit and veg sellers can catch you off guard, almost making you jump as you walk by. They attempt to push segments of clementine into your hands, knowing full well that once you've tasted one, it will be difficult to resist a purchase. Then there are the rainbow-coloured flower stands that burst in spring with rows of fluffy white, cotton-candy-pink or fuchsia-pink peonies. The markets are a sight to behold, and certainly one of my favourite aspects of living in the French capital.

Paris markets to know

Le Marché Bastille – I hold a soft spot for Le Marché Bastille, as it's the market that I used to visit every Sunday to buy my weekly food. It's also one of the city's largest markets, spreading over the covered area of the city's canal towards Place de la Bastille. During my Sunday pilgrimage to the market, I would also pick up a plate of oysters for 6.50€, a plastic cup of Muscadet for 2.50€ (which also washes down nicely with oysters), and a bag of hot *accras de morue* (battered spiced balls of salted cod) from the adjacent stall, which specialised in food from Martinque. This is one of my favourite aspects about Parisian markets: you can find a stall of oysters hailing from Brittany in the northeast of France next to food from an island off the coast of Africa – wildly different foods, but both decidedly Parisian.

Marché Aligre – Marché Beauveau, or Marché Aligre as it's usually called, due to its location running along Rue d'Aligre in the 12th arrondissement, is positioned to the east of Place de la Bastille and is divided into two sections – an outdoor and indoor space. The indoor market (historically called Marché Beauveau) is housed in a large tile-roofed hall and is home to Hardouin-Langlet *fromagerie*, which makes the market worth a visit just for its staggering amount of different cheeses – 350, according to a review by *Le Figaro* in 2013. Outside, stalls set up camp six days a week (Tuesday–Sunday) on the square situated to the east of the covered area, along Rue d'Aligre towards Rue du Faubourg Saint-Antoine. Here, you'll also find Café Aouba coffee shop and café, which has been on this site since 1938.

Les Enfants Rouge – Located on the site of an old sixteenth-century orphanage, this market owes its name to the orphaned children who lived there – they wore red clothes donated by Christian charities. Les Enfants Rouges is Paris's sole fully covered market, and the only one that I do in fact go to simply to mooch around, eat lunch and be seen. I love nothing more than to wander through the aisles and order freshly made sandwiches, a bento box filled with tempura chicken and rice from Plat Bento, or a portion of lamb tagine from Le Traiteur

Morocain. There's also a very good French brasserie called L'Estaminet des Enfants inside the market that serves great *confit de canard*.

Marché Dejean – Marché Dejean is a sprawling market located in the Goutte d'Or area in the 18th arrondissement. It's known as *la petite Afrique* (Little Africa), as it cuts across a pedestrianised street that's home to a multitude of African hair salons, tailors and fabric shops. There, among the fruit and veg, you will find tilapia, a fish important to artisanal fishing in Africa; bissap, a species of hibiscus native to areas of Africa; and manioc, a root vegetable that is considered a hero of African cuisine. This is the market to visit if you want to get the

full, unadulterated experience of Paris's food scene – it's a different taste of Paris, but one that is integral to the city's culinary landscape and history.

Marché Rungis – You'll need a 'buyers card' to get in (or a friend with one) as this is for wholesalers only, but if you're feeling particularly brave and are more interested in the produce than the traditional picturesque Parisian setting, then Rungis is the place to go. It's the largest wholesale market in the world, spanning an enormous 232 hectares. It also boasts an enormous offering of plants and flowers. It's best to go early to get your hands on the best produce.

⚜

What to buy at a Parisian market

Of course, there are many things you can buy at a market, and really the best thing is to go and to try as much as you can for yourself. But there are a few items that I always have on my shopping list.

Fish – like whole sea bass, salmon fillets and fresh prawns
Whole rotisserie chicken – great if you're planning on cooking a roast, as then you only have to make the accompaniments
Cheese – Saint Felician, Comté and Parmesan

Fresh flowers – tulips and peonies in spring and
wreaths at Christmas time

Fruit and vegetables – Lettuce, artichokes, mushroom
varieties, tomatoes, pomegranates, herbs and fresh
orange juice

Poitrine **(pork belly)** – for lardons

And finally: lunch! – Eat oysters straight from the
stalls in the months they're in season. The sellers
will open them in front of you and serve them on
a dedicated plastic oyster plate for six or twelve.
Purchase a cup of wine (often Muscadet) to go
with them. You can also buy a bag of *accra*.
Alternatively, pick up a small quiche and then a
Nutella-filled crêpe for dessert.

⚜

Essential items & ingredients for a Parisian-inspired kitchen

— Dijon mustard and à l'Ancienne (wholegrain)
   mustard

— Salted butter – *demi-sel* in French

— A good natural full fat yogurt

— Green lettuce – for your French vinaigrette and green
   salad side dish

— Bottle of wine – white (Sancerre, Pouilly-Fumé or
   Petit Chablis) and red (Côtes du Rhône)

— Garlic
— Herbs – thyme, rosemary, mint, coriander, basil
  (depending on what's in season)
— Comté and Roquefort cheese
— Cream
— Reblochon in winter (for tartiflette)
— Eggs
— Red wine vinegar
— Olive oil
— Fleur de sel – a type of salt
— Lardons – preferably bought whole as *poitrine*, then
  cut into lardons by hand at home
— Bread – *baguette tradition*
— Good ground coffee (or beans if you have a grinder)
— Mariage Frères tea
— Good Italian pasta (linguine)
— Seasonal fruit and vegetables
— Shallots, onions and potatoes (all year round)

Bread & pâtisseries

'With enough butter, anything is good'
Julia Child

There is nothing more stereotypically French than popping out to your local *boulangerie* and picking up a buttery croissant for breakfast on the weekend. Yet they really do it. And, in case you're wondering, Parisians also queue outside *boulangeries* daily for fresh bread. I mention this because, although I've become accustomed to this phenomenon over the past eight years, it's still one of my favourite sights to see in the city, and I notice it every time I walk past a queue. It's one of the rituals that I've come to love about Paris – and they're the only queues I don't mind joining.

Frank Barron's top three *pâtisseries* to try next time you're in Paris

Frank (@cakeboyparis), who is originally from the US, is a brilliant baker and cake decorator. He hosts baking workshops (and is now writing a book), but he is also a purveyor of good style and interiors taste (take a peek at his enviable Marais apartment on Instagram). Knowing that he's an expert in all things sweet and baked in Paris, I asked him to name his favourite *pâtisseries*.

The Croissant Ispahan by Pierre Hermé

I would cross the river just to pick up Pierre Hermé's signature croissant. It's a classic flaky, buttery croissant, glazed with a rose-flavoured almond cream, topped with candied rose petals and filled with a delectable raspberry, rose and lychee paste. Pick one up at his Rue Bonaparte boutique and enjoy on a park bench in the nearby Luxembourg Gardens.

Le Mont Blanc from Angelina

The Mont Blanc is one of my favourite French pastries, and the best one in the city is also the original. The recipe at Angelina has remained unchanged since it was created in 1903. I love the different textures: crunchy French meringue wrapped in the lightest whipped cream, covered in sweet chestnut paste. I usually treat myself to one during winter with a big pot of tea or a cup of Angelina's famous hot chocolate.

Le Fraisier by Mori Yoshida

A *fraisier* is a traditional French pastry composed primarily of

genoise sponge cake, strawberries and whipped cream.
I love the Japanese approach to the design of this *pâtisserie*,
and the abundance of chantilly whipped cream sandwiched
between the lightest sponge cake I have ever tasted. A perfect
summertime treat in Paris!

Parisian café culture & coffee

'When I sit in Paris in a café, surrounded by people,
I don't sit casually – I go over a certain sonata in
my head and discover new things all the time'
Arthur Rubinstein

Café culture is an aspect of Paris life that marries the city's social traditions with its long history of art, literature and politics. It is an integral part of what it means to be Parisian – cafés are the beating hearts of many arrondissements. In some cases, they almost act as second living rooms to the city's inhabitants. As I explained in the

Interiors & Home Life chapter, space is at a premium in Paris and apartments can be tiny, so residents will often spill into cafés and restaurants to meet friends. Although their image has been updated thanks to a flurry of new coffee shops that have sprung up over the past ten to fifteen years, they are also what helps to perpetuate the romanticised Parisian lifestyle, as Lindsey Tramuta pointed out in her book *The New Paris*: 'the café space is key to understanding the idealised Parisian experience and the mythology around it'. It's an impression that was confirmed when I was talking to one of my oldest friends from the UK during the coronavirus pandemic, when travel was restricted. She exclaimed that one of the things she missed most was hopping on the Eurostar to Paris and whiling away a few hours in a café whilst watching the world go by through the window.

There is no scene more classically or stereotypically Parisian than that of the writer sitting in a café or on its terrace, pen in one hand and coffee in the other, writing down their musings as the world passes by. This image was made famous by the likes of Ernest Hemingway, who wrote his debut book, *The Sun Also Rises*, in a Parisian café – namely Le Select in Montparnasse, which was also a favourite haunt of Pablo Picasso and F. Scott Fitzgerald in the 1920s. And legend has it that Fitzgerald read the manuscript of *The Great Gatsby* to Hemingway in Café Closerie de Lilas. To explain why cafés were (and still are) so important to the daily lives of Parisians, I will give a bit of historical context.

Paris has been renowned for its café culture since the seventeenth century, when Francesco Procopio dei Coltelli, an Italian chef, opened Café Procope in 1686 in the 6th arrondissement, a few feet from Boulevard Saint Germain. It's widely considered Paris's oldest café in continuous operation (although it had a hiatus from 1872 until the 1920s). Today it's a restaurant, and a key landmark for anyone visiting the city, who wants to know what it feels like to dine in a 400-year-old establishment. The café's opening was the catalyst for a new era of consumption and socialising that also helped level the playing field between classes, as Tramuta writes, in reference to W. Scott Haine's book *The World of the Paris Café*: 'The café became a safe, comforting haven during periods of unrest – a hotbed of conversation, political thought, writing and sharing beliefs publicly.' This idea of the café not being purely a place for a shot of caffeine, but an important space for human connection is exactly what Fanny Flory, co-founder of one of Paris's relatively new cafés, Passager, attests to when I chat to her on page 300 – it is what she loves most about owning a café in Paris.

When I moved to Paris eight years ago, the tide had already turned. The old-style cafés, stuffier remnants of Paris's past and the roaring twenties, although beautiful and still frequented by locals and tourists alike, were waning in popularity with the advent of a new wave of cosier coffee shops, dedicated to good coffee. Their founders were generally foreign or Parisian upstarts who had learned the art of a good brew abroad, namely in Australia or the US. They began updating Paris's coffee offerings, which up until the mid-2000s had been, according to Tramuta, mainly bitter espresso brewed from beans that were often stale. The first to open was Caféothèque, in 2005; it was the first of its kind and helped inspire the city's 'third-wave coffee movement', which followed a few years later. Caféothèque was launched as a self-professed 'temple of coffee', and its owner, Gloria Montenegro, a former Ambassador for Guatemala, approached coffee in the same way as the French approach wine, offering a huge variety of different beans from various coffee-producing countries.

As I began diving into Parisian life in 2013, cafés did indeed become my second living room, and often also my office space as I joined other freelancers with my laptop in places like KB Café in the 9th arrondissement, which opened in 2010. Back in London I had been a dedicated tea-drinker and was consuming, at my peak, four to five cups a day. But upon moving to the French capital, I soon swapped my tea habit for a coffee one. With fresh-off-the-boat eagerness and a little more time on my hands, I even made it my mission in my early Paris days to visit every new café that was springing up in the capital. They were also, incidentally, the places where I met most of my blogging friends after connecting through Instagram.

While my interest in visiting every new café has dwindled, I still consider them 'destinations' and love nothing more than meeting a friend in one on the weekend. Café culture, albeit a changed one is still very much a part of Parisian life as it was when Hemingway was here. They were also one of the main things I missed most, besides bars and restaurants of course, during the confinements, as what, I mused, is living in Paris without being able to while away a few hours in a café watching the world go by?

Yasmin Zeinab's favourite places to get coffee in Paris

Yasmin (@sundaysinparis) is an author and expat from Australia, who has been living in Paris since 2018. She published her second book, a city guide to Marrakesh, in early 2021. As a fellow café and good coffee aficionado, I asked her to tell me her favourite spots in Paris for a great brew.

Café Kitsune, inside Palais Royal

Set in the beautiful and historic Palais-Royal, this Café Kitsune outpost is my favourite place in the city for coffee. In the warmer months, I love to sit on the café's terrace, set under Palais Royal's perfectly manicured trees, or lounge by the fountain on one of the iconic green garden chairs. The coffee is exceptional, and you can't go wrong with one of their gluten-free cookies or a *financier*.

Circus Bakery

Opened in 2018 by the team behind Fragments (a coveted café in the 3rd arrondissement), Circus is home to Paris's best cinnamon bun. Behind a charming store front in the city's Latin Quarter, the bare bones space is small and has limited seating, a couple of long benches nestled amongst crates of fresh fruit, so you may need to order your coffee to go. When I was based on the Left Bank, I would venture here every Saturday morning for a cinnamon bun and an *allongée* (black coffee). Everything that comes out of the oven here is outstanding, but the cinnamon bun is a must-order (especially when they're freshly baked).

Beans on Fire

Tucked away in the heart of the 11th arrondissement on a leafy cul-de-sac, Beans on Fire is my go-to spot for my morning coffee. A neighbourhood favourite, it's often bustling with locals basking in the sun on the sprawling outdoor terrace that overlooks a charming park (Square Gardette). The quality of the coffee here is hard to beat, and the setting is perfect for watching daily life in Paris go by.

A chat about café life with Fanny Flory

Fanny (@fannyb) is a former stylist turned Influencer, who opened Passager café in the 11th arrondissement a few years ago with a friend. It was my go-to spot when I lived in the area, and so I thought she would be the perfect person to chat to about café life in Paris.

Why did you open a café?

It was by total coincidence. I met my future associate, who already had a restaurant in the 11th when I was writing about addresses of note for a magazine. We hit it off and would have coffees together from time to time. I also helped him with his social platforms. One day he asked if I wanted to open a café together. The area surrounding Rue de Charonne in the 11th was missing a good one, so we decided to open Passager there.

Why do you think cafés, café culture and coffee are so important to Parisian life?

Cafés are important to help one reconnect with what's essential in life and for the atmosphere that exists in these places. Go into a café, order your favourite coffee and drink it with a book or with a friend, while observing Parisian life through the windows. Chat with the people sitting at the table next to you, and finish by eating a slice of cake. They are simple things, but do you the world of good.

How have you seen café culture change in the last few years?

At the beginning, I found that the food in cafés didn't always match the quality of the coffee. We drank good coffee, but the food was not very good. In recent years, things have changed; the coffee experience now is to drink good coffee *and* eat well. Good work has gone into the food in the last few years, and the pastries are getting better and better! Cafés have their place in catering all day long: from morning until early evening.

What's your favourite thing about owning a café in Paris?

It reconnected me to a 'human' profession: meeting people, putting the world to rights: seeing a lot of different people is very enriching. It's a working environment that doesn't make you worry.

❧

ADDRESS BOOK

Classic Bistros
Aux Prés *(25 Rue du Dragon, 75006)*
Bistro Paul Bert *(18 Rue Paul Bert, 75011)*
Bouillon Chartier *(7 Rue du Faubourg Montmartre, 75009)*
Café Constant *(139 Rue Saint-Dominique, 75007)*
Café des Musées *(49 Rue de Turenne, 75003)*
Chez Georges *(1 Rue du Mail, 75002)*
Le Chardenoux *(1 Rue Jules Vallès, 75011)*
Le Petit Marché *(9 Rue de Béarn, 75003)*

Modern/Neo Bistros
Le 5 Paul Bert *(6 Rue Paul-Bert Paris, 75011)*
Abri *(92 Rue du Faubourg-Poissonnière, 75010)*
Au Passage *(1 bis Saint-Sébastien, 75001)*
Carbon *(14 Rue Charlot, 75003)*
Clown Bar *(114 Rue Amelot, 75011)*
Ellsworth *(34 Rue Richelieu, 75001)*
Pierre Sang *(6 Rue Gambey, 75011)*
Le Servan *(32 Rue Saint-Maur, 75011)*

Caves à manger (wine bars and small plates)
Aux Deux Amis *(45 Rue Oberkampf, 75011)*
Bambino *(25 Rue Saint-Sébastien, 75011)*
Brutal *(3 Rue Eugène Carrière, 75018)*
La Buvette *(67 Rue Saint-Maur, 75011)*

Le Dauphin *(131 Avenue Parmentier, 75011)*
Frenchie Bar à Vins *(6 Rue du Nil, 75002)*
Martin *(24 Boulevard du Temple, 75011)*
Le Mary Celeste *(1 Rue Commines, 75003)*
Septime la Cave *(3 Rue Basfroi, 75011)*
Le Verre Volé *(67 Rue de Lancry, 75010)*
Yard Cave *(6 Rue de Mont-Louis, 75011)*

Modern tasting menus
Comice *(31 Avenue de Versailles, 75016)*
Frenchie *(5–6 Rue du Nil, 75002)*
Septime *(80 Rue de Charonne, 75011)*
Verjus *(52 Rue de Richelieu, 75001)*

Old, classic cafés/brasseries
Café de Flore *(172 Boulevard Saint-Germain, 75006)*
La Closerie des Lilas *(171 Boulevard du
    Montparnasse, 75006)*
Les Deux Magots *(6 Place Saint-Germain des Prés,
    75006)*
Le Select *(99 Boulevard du Montparnasse, 75006)*

Good coffee
Boot Café *(19 Rue du Pont aux Choux, 75003)*
Café Craft *(24 Rue des Vinaigriers, 75010)*
Café Lomi *(3 Ter Rue Marcadet, 75018)*
Café Loustic *(40 Rue Chapon, 75003)*
Café Kitsune Tuileries *(208 Rue de Rivoli, 75001)*
Café Oberkampf *(3 Rue Neuve Popincourt, 75011)*
The Caféothèque of Paris *(52 Rue de l'Hôtel de ville,
    75004)*

Caoua *(98 Quai de Jemmapes, 75010)*

Coutume Café *(47 Rue de Babylone, 75007)*

KB Cafeshop *(53 Rue Avenue Trudaine, 75009)*

Ob La Di *(54 Rue de Saintonge, 75003)*

Passager *(107 Avenue Ledru Rollin, 75011)*

Le Peleton Café *(17 Rue du Pont Louis-Philippe,*
75004)

Shakespeare & Company Café *(37 Rue de la Bûcherie,*
75005)

Télescope *(5 Rue Villédo, 75001)*

Ten Belles *(10 Rue de la Grange aux Belles, 75010)*

Artisanal *boulangeries/pâtisseries* and other
sweet treats

Circus – artisanal bakery and coffee *(63 Rue Galande,*
75005)

Liberté – artisanal bakery *(39 Rue des Vinaigriers,*
75010)

Chambelland – gluten-free bakery *(14 Rue Ternaux,*
75011)

Colorova – *pâtisserie* and café *(47 Rue de l'Abbé*
Grégoire, 75006)

La Chocolaterie – *pâtisserie* and chocolate shop *(25*
Rue Chanzy, 75011)

La Pâtisserie Cyril Lignac *(24 Rue Paul Bert, 75011)*

Une Glace a Paris – ice cream *(15 Rue Sainte-Croix de*
la Bretonnerie, 75004)

Mori Yoshida – *pâtisserie (65 Avenue de Breteuil,*
75007 Paris)

Yann Couvreur – *pâtisserie (www.yanncouvreur.com)*
Popelini – puffed (choux) pastry filled with cream
   (popelini.com)

International
116 – Japanese *(2 Rue Auguste Vacquerie, 75116)*
Balagan – Israeli *(9 Rue d'Alger, 75001)*
Bazurto – Colombian *(5 Rue de L'Ancienne, 75006)*
CAM – Chinese *(55 Rue au Maire, 75003)*
Double Dragon – Chinese *(52 Rue Saint-Maur, 75011)*
Kunitoraya – Japanese specialising in udon noodles
   (1 Rue Villédo, 75001)
Miznon – Israeli *(22 Rue des Ecouffes, 75004)*
Le Petit Pékin – Chinese *(162 Avenue Parmentier,
   75010)*
Pink Mamma – Italian *(20 bis Rue de Douai, 75009)*
SAaM – Korean fusion *(59 bis Rue de Lancry, 75010)*
El Vecino – Mexican *(13 Boulevard du Temple, 75003)*

Seafood
Clamato *(80 Rue de Charonne, 75011)*
Fichon *(98 Rue Marcadet, 75018)*
Huguette *(81 Rue de Seine, 75006)*
Sur Mer *(53 Rue de Lancry, 75010)*

Cocktail bars
Bisou *(15 Boulevard de Temple, 75003)*
Candelaria *(52 Rue de Saintonge, 75003)*
Dirty Lemon *(24 Rue de la Folie Méricourt, 75011)*
Experimental Cocktail Club *(37 Rue Saint-Sauveur,
   75002)*

Frequence *(20 Rue Keller, 75011)*
Little Red Door *(60 Rue Charlot, 75003)*
Lulu White *(12 Rue Frochot, 75009)*
Serpent à Plume *(24 Place des Vosges, 75003)*
Sherry Butt *(20 Rue Beautreillis, 75004)*

Healthy/vegan
Jah Jah by Le Tricycle *(11 Rue des Petites Écuries, 75010)*
Kitchen *(74 Rue des Gravilliers, 75003)*
Sol Semilla *(23 Rue des Vinaigriers, 75010)*
Wild & the Moon *(www.wildandthemoon.fr)*

Relationships, love & dating

The city of love

'La valeur suprême in France is passion'
**Elodie Fagan, senior marketing and
communications manager for Tinder France**

By now you'll know that I moved to Paris for love, yet
stayed when the relationship ended. You might have also
realised that while I was writing this book, I fell in love
with a Parisian – rather fortuitously, too, as there's no
better way to learn (and write) about how to be a little
more Parisian than to date one, even
after eight years of living in the city. As
I write, I have been in a relationship
for the past few months with a man
who grew up in the 15th arrondissement. Ninety-five per cent of our
communication is in French.

Much like moving to Paris,
this was not part of my
original life plan. I love
Parisians, and my admi-
ration of their way of life,
their style, their city and
their culture all form part
of why I wanted to write

this book. However, perhaps surprisingly, I never actually wanted to date a man who was born in Paris. Let's just say that Parisian men have something of a bad reputation for having inflated egos (and that's according to French Parisians and expats alike). When I threw myself back into the world of dating in early September 2020, I generally sought out men from smaller cities, like Bordeaux, Lille, Lyon or perhaps Dijon – men without (or so I thought) the pretentions that can come with being born and raised in the world's most beautiful city.

Yet here I am, in a relationship with a Parisian man, and I couldn't be happier. True to form, he has opinions on everything from food to fashion. During our first conversation, he told me, very matter-of-factly, that he didn't really like London (something I've come to respect about the Parisians is that they're nothing if not upfront and honest). He insists that men shouldn't wear shorts in a city, especially in Paris (the same goes for flip flops), and claims you cannot truly be Parisian until you want to move out of Paris. He lives in Montreuil, one of the up-and-coming suburbs on the other side of the *Périphérique*, the motorway that encircles Paris like a fence, separating what some might deem the 'real Paris' and its arrondissements from the *banlieue* (suburbs). This word is often used disparagingly: many Paris-born Parisians feel that if you grew up in the *banlieue*, you are not a true Parisian. Ironically, however, many Parisians now want to move there to take advantage of more space and escape the noise of the city . . . Yes, they are nothing if not contradictory.

But I digress. Despite all these opinions and preferences, he has turned out to be the kindest, most loving man I've been with since my first love – and he has taught me more about romance and relationships than most of my previous boyfriends did.

But it took me some time to find him, and the three years I spent dating in Paris gave me a lot of insight into the ways that Parisians approach love, sex, dating (both IRL and online) and relationships. After befriending many Parisians and navigating the dating scene here, I have come to learn that, as with the other areas of life I have written about in this book, Parisians do things a little differently when it comes to matters of the heart. For example: passion is paramount, they are quicker to embrace love, they are more liberated when it comes to sex, and marriage isn't always the end goal. I believe my dating experiences in Paris have helped me to forge better relationships, and allowed me to go after what I actually want rather than what I think I should be pursuing based on societal pressures. Of course, in this chapter, I am speaking from my own experiences, as a heterosexual woman dating men. Whatever your romantic situation, I hope that some of the lessons I've learned might help make your own dating experiences and relationships better, too.

We'll always have Paris

'Just add three letters to Paris, and you have paradise'
Jules Renard

Paris is often regarded as the romantic capital of the world: a city that has been synonymous with love and romance for centuries. Even the French language is deemed romantic to the ear (I concur). Many couples come to Paris for a romantic weekend away, and some people even travel here to propose to their loved one under the twinkly lights of the Eiffel Tower. It's common here to see loved-up couples (French and foreign) strolling hand in hand along the Seine, snuggling up at tiny

brasserie tables on terraces or stopping on a bridge to admire the view and share a passionate kiss.

This link between Paris and romance is partly thanks to the city's beauty, but it's also due to French philosophy and historical literature, as well as films like *Sabrina*, *Funny Face* and 1942's *Casablanca*, in which Humphrey Bogart famously bids farewell to Ingrid Bergman with the bittersweet line: 'We'll always have Paris.' More recent films have perpetuated this image of Paris as the world's most romantic city, including *Before Sunset*, *Paris je t'aime* and *French Kiss*, and it's a reputation that's further fuelled by the flood of Instagram snaps of couples posing by some of the city's most famous landmarks – photo shoots that many Paris-based photographers now make a living from, because they are in such high demand. These things, and many others, have helped put Paris on the map as *the* destination for a romantic getaway.

And it's not just an outside interpretation – the French really do love love. Having lived here for nearly a decade, I completely agree with American feminist and historian Marilyn Yam, who states in her book *How the French Invented Love*: '[Love] occupies a privileged place in their national identity, on a par with fashion, food and human rights.' This sentiment was confirmed by my French friend Magali Gnocchi when I spoke to her for this section: '*Je suis amoureuse de l'amour.*' ('I am in love with love.'). Parisians love fiercely, easily and passionately.

A 2019 report on love in the digital age written by the French advertising and communications agency Havas

Group placed the French in the 'Passionates' category (along with Italians, Belgians and the Dutch), meaning that to them 'love is an end in itself – a passionate adventure that sparks excitement and pleasure. In these countries, seduction tends to be considered an art, and romance is vital to one's sense of self.' This is in contrast to the more 'goal-orientated' countries categorised as 'Achievers', such as the UK, USA, Poland and Portugal, where 'love is seen as a means to an end. One seeks out and commits to a love relationship in order to forge a lifelong partnership and create a family unit.' This is not to say that the French and the Parisians don't also want lifelong partnership and families, but they are more interested in the journey than the end goal. In my opinion, this is a healthier approach. This idea is reiterated by Deborah Oliver in her book, *What French Women Know*: 'the French are groomed to think about love from an early age . . . not in the absolutes of total love or utter rejection, but in nuances and a range of possibilities. It dawned on me . . . that while we Americans are groomed to seek happy endings and closure, the French are more comfortable with emotional subtleties and ambiguity. While we grow up thinking about love in black and white, they grow up inscrutably grey.'

I would certainly agree that it is the journey – the romance and passion – that takes precedence here in Paris. It's something I've noticed when dating other French men, as well as in my current relationship. This makes me feel a little freer. I feel less of the social constraints that I felt while living in the UK. Perhaps this is why, as I wrote in the introduction, Paris has been the perfect place for me to explore my interests. I feel less pressure here to be married, have a mortgage and have kids by a certain age.

Ten things I've learned about love & relationships from being in a relationship with a Parisian

1. Have opinions and don't be afraid to express them – Parisians love to talk, debate, critique and discuss everything from what cheese should be brought to an *apéro* to whether or not they should breastfeed their children. They are big readers, love watching films – especially French films, which are usually based on the topics of sex, relationships and existential musings on the meaning of life, with not a lot actually happening – and they absorb culture, frequently going to museums and art exhibitions. So, of course, they have opinions on everything. Discussing your opinions is an important part of keeping a relationship interesting and alive, even if you don't agree with each other (in fact, this can sometimes be more advantageous, as it encourages you both to consider different viewpoints). If you feel you are somewhat lacking in the opinion department, watch more documentaries and read more – biographies, books on history and, dare I say, *The Second Sex* by Simone de Beauvoir. Think about the points being raised in these books and decide if you agree.

2. Sex is one of the most important things in your relationship – You must make time for sex. You could even, as Esther Perel promotes, schedule it! There is nothing wrong with planning exactly when to have sex with your partner. In fact it can be exciting, because you have it to look forward to. Also, a healthy sex life is an important part of many relationships, and it's important to communicate about it if you feel like things aren't right in this department.

3. Tell your partner when they do something that makes you happy – This might sound like common sense, but I think it's something that is easily forgotten in relationships. If you can get into the habit from the beginning of praising your partner when they do something that makes you happy, then great, but it's something that can also be introduced later down the line. It's just a mindset that needs adopting. Not only will it make them feel happy and appreciated, but it will encourage them to do it more. And it's much better to point out the good than the bad. For example, if your partner rarely does the laundry, but decides to do it on a Saturday morning, then praise the fact they're doing it rather than pointing out that they almost never do it.

4. Don't be afraid of confrontation – At the same time, if there is something your partner has said or done that has upset you or you don't agree with, do not be afraid to speak your mind. Choose a good time to chat, when neither one of you is busy or working, and take time to air out the issue. This can actually bring you closer together.

5. Remember your flaws are what make you lovable – Admittedly, I've always been in the 'striving for perfection' camp. I've always put a lot of pressure on myself and don't like to show my weaknesses or flaws. But because Parisians don't spotlight perfection and tend to see imperfections as more interesting, it has helped me to be more accepting of my own, and I am no longer afraid to show them.

6. Do not smother your partner or put undue pressure on them – Give them the freedom to be and do what they want (within your value system and boundaries of course), as you would want the same treatment from them. It's a trivial example, but if they love an activity or sport like football and you don't, just vacate the room and find something else to do while it's on, or leave them to watch a match with friends. And never go into a relationship thinking you can change something about the other person further down the line. If they don't do or enjoy something now, it's unlikely that they will later.

7. A relationship should be an equal partnership – You are not two halves making up a whole – you are two complete individuals choosing to come together to pursue a life together.

8. Leave a little to the imagination – Familiarity can sometimes make us take our partner for granted. Always leave a little to the imagination. Of course you can get cosy and comfortable, but preserving some things for yourself helps to keep a relationship alive and exciting.

9. Put your happiness first – They might be your favourite person, but you must remain number one and should always prioritise your own happiness. Relation-ships always involve compromise, but you should not be compromising so much that it makes you miserable. On the flip side, you should always state when you need your partner to compromise on something that is impor-tant to you. A relationship should involve give and take – and balance. As Proust wrote in *Pastiches et Mélanges*: 'When you work to please others you can't succeed, but the things you do to satisfy yourself stand a chance of catching someone's interest.'

10. Enjoy the moment – Of course you can make plans for the future, but don't focus solely on them. You never know where the future may take you, and you need to keep an open mind and attitude. I am certainly testament to that. Enjoy where you are right now.

Sophie Trem's tips for maintaining a healthy relationship

Sophie (@theotherartofliving) is a digital consultant and the creator of the blog The Other Art of Living. She also founded The Good Mood Class, a series of workshops and resources (and now also a book) to boost wellbeing and positive thinking. She also co-founded Good Mood Dealer, a brand that creates products and books focused on spirituality and self-development. She met her husband at eighteen: they took a one-year break at the age of twenty-one, married at twenty-five and have been together for twenty-three years. They have two boys, aged eight and twelve, and live between Paris and Normandy. Here are Sophie's tips for a healthy relationship.

Say exactly what you feel, even if it leads to an argument
We used to argue all the time when we were younger – I've always been very hot-blooded, and if there was something that angered me, I had a hard time keeping quiet. While I've since grown and mellowed, I do think that to say what you really feel would be the most important thing to me. Plus, you should never do something just to make the other person happy. When you try to organise the relationship too much, you are not living it mindfully. It's important to do things for the person you love, but it's also important that it makes you happy, too. If you feel like it's a duty, it's not a good sign.

Sometimes we think that the other person expects something from us, but most of the time this is not the case. And most of the time, the other person doesn't know that we don't like it. This is the problem for 90 per cent of the population – that everyone thinks that we all think in the same way, but in fact we each have our own truth, and it isn't the same for everyone.

Be careful about asking for advice
Most people worry too much about what others are going to say and think. You have to make sure your family and friends don't influence your decisions too much. You can ask for advice, but remember they are not living the relationship, and they don't know everything. Most of the time, when you ask for advice the other person will reflect their own expectations and fears back at you.

Listen to your body and pay attention to how you feel
Your body can tell you a lot about your mental wellbeing. If you have a pain somewhere, it means that your spirit and body are not aligned. Pain is a message – your body is telling you that you are not going in the right direction. For example, pain in your liver suggests anger. Emotions can get stuck in your body. Most of the time when you think about relationships, you think with your head and your heart (within your vocabulary). But you should only listen to yourself – your true self and how you feel. It's about trusting your intuition.

Maintain your own life
I love my family, but I think it's very important to have breathing space, purpose and dreams outside of the family unit. You don't have to choose between being one thing or another. I'm a mother, a wife and a family member, and I'm also myself. Most people think that they have to compromise on everything. You have to create

balance and sometimes compromise, but I think you can do it all – just differently. You should never feel like you're abandoning what you love for the sake of a relationship or having a family.

Make projects together
One of the most important things is to create dreams and make plans together. It's like seeing a chain of mountains and aiming for the highest one.

Sex & seduction

'To a Frenchman, sex provides the most
economical way to have fun'
Anita Loos

When it comes to sex, the French have a long-standing reputation for not only having more of it and being great at it (let us not forget they invented the French kiss), but also for having a much more liberated approach to it (the last point I certainly agree with). This reputation derives from their royal history (where everyone seemed to be having salacious affairs) and their literature. A classic example is the book *Les Liaisons Dangereuses*, which was published in 1782 and tells the story of ex-lovers who use their skills of seduction to manipulate and exploit others. It has been adapted to film a few times, most famously as *Cruel Intentions*, starring Reese Witherspoon. And then there's the likes of *Chéri*, published in 1920, which depicts a love affair between an older woman and a younger man. It was written by the Nobel Prize-nominated author Sidonie-Gabrielle Colette, known simply as Colette. Widely acknowledged as one of France's most talented writers, Colette (described as 'promiscuous in art and love' by the *Guardian*) wrote about love, sex and relationships. And, of course, it would be impossible to consider the French attitude to love and sex without looking to Simone de Beauvoir's seminal work *The Second Sex*, which not only fuelled feminism and helped liberate women, but also negatively portrayed marriage, defended abortion and encouraged women to take younger lovers. It's also worth pointing out that Paris is home to the world-famous Moulin Rouge, the cabaret where the modern-day version of the can-can was born – originally introduced as a seductive dance by courtesans who were operating on the site in Pigalle, the city's red light district.

This reputation for having a more liberated and passionate approach to romance continues to be reinforced today – for example, in the Netflix show *Emily in Paris*, one of the characters declares : 'You haven't done Paris right until you've had at least one wildly inappropriate affair.' Of course, this series bolsters a lot of bad clichés, but on this front, I think they got it right. This is something my friend Magali Gnocchi confirmed when I chatted to her: 'When I was travelling, I heard that Paris is called the "city of sex", and it's true. If you want to have sex, you can – it's very easy here. Guys can flirt with girls, and we're okay with it. We are more straightforward. We love to flirt, to seduce, and we like to please other people.'

And, of course, it's a reputation the French themselves continue to propagate. In an interview with the *Wall Street Journal*, fashion journalist and author Sophie Fontanel said: 'In France, we have a reputation . . . We are the country of eroticism.' Ironically, she was being interviewed about her book *L'Envie*, which documents her experiences of abstaining from sex for more than a decade, but it's important to point out that she didn't set out to abstain from sex per se: she was rebelling against bad sex, and this just happened to turn into twelve years of no sex at all. She wasn't prudish or closed-minded: she simply didn't want to waste time having bad sex. And, according to James Wolcott, writing in *Vanity Fair* in 2013, Fontanel even managed to make giving up sex sound sexy: 'Leave it to a Frenchwoman to convert giving up sex into an elegant gesture that reeks of worldliness and sends up a smoky wreath.'

Loud & proud

'Là où il y a de la gêne il n'y a pas de plaisir'
('Where there's shame, there's no pleasure')
French proverb

I'm afraid I cannot confirm if the French definitely have more sex (and I will keep you guessing about whether they are indeed better), but something I can tell you that I've discovered since living in Paris is that there is less of a taboo surrounding sex. There's less shame (refer to the proverb above), they are more than likely to have sex sooner because it is so crucial to the quality of their relationships, and, in my experience (from living in various apartments in Paris), they make more noise when doing it. There's that famous scene in the film *Amélie*, where she sits on the roof of her building and wonders how many people are simultaneously reaching climax. I remember thinking it was rather funny and bold of the director to include that scene, and I probably blushed when I watched it. Then I moved to Paris. Of course, it might simply be down to the lack of space and the fact that Parisians are packed rather tightly into apartments where the walls are thin, but I have never lived in a city where I've heard so much sex. I've heard it through the walls, coming up through the floorboards and on hot days, when the windows are open . . . well, you can imagine. In one studio apartment that I lived in in La Marais, I used to hear it so much that I even started *imagining* that I was hearing it.

The conclusion I've come to is that it's not necessarily that the French have more sex, or even that they are better lovers: I think they are just better at being honest about it, talking about it in their relationships and not hiding it. This could also explain why they are less worried about making noise while they do it – after all, it's a natural act!

I would argue that, rather than necessarily being 'better' lovers, what they are better at is just being more human about it and not allowing feelings of shame to get in the way. As my friend Magali also pointed out to me: 'We are more liberated, perhaps. There is less shame. And the pursuit of pleasure is part of our lifestyle.'

Dating: there is no French word for 'date'

'We believe that the magic of love is when two people meet thanks to little coincidences, and when an unpredictable alchemy makes them connect and really fit together'
Didier Rappaport, CEO of Happn

In the April of 2018, following the break-up of a long-term relationship, I threw myself into online dating with the same gusto as one might a new hobby. I'd almost say that it did become a new hobby of sorts, especially at the beginning when I started chatting to and meeting new men. I had never done it before, and was bemused by how, with just one swipe, you could be in conversation with a man you'd never met. I found it fascinating, intriguing and I was keen to give it a good go. Having missed the boat, so to speak, in London, I was like a kid in a candy store. Of course, the novelty wore off, as anyone will know if they've experienced it; the landscape of online dating is not easy to navigate, and I was also grappling with a different culture and language that was not my own. But I treated it like a tool, and while it was sometimes challenging, it was certainly eye-opening. During my three years of dating, which included one short relationship, I learned a lot about myself, and also about how the Parisians 'date' – or, more accurately, how they don't, because here in Paris, 'dating' isn't something that happens in the same way – or as frequently – as it does in cities like London or New York, for example.

Dating is a relatively new concept in France. They are not big 'daters' (and by that I mean they don't tend to see multiple people romantically at the same time), because it doesn't really fit in with the way in which they approach love and finding a meaningful relationship. They prefer to meet a significant other *par hazard* (by chance), perhaps through work, via friends of friends, or in real-life social situations, e.g. at a party or in a bar. Dating and online dating are still quite new territory here, and Parisians tend to approach them differently. Most of the Parisians I've spoken to don't like online dating because it takes away the opportunity of a 'chance meeting', instead turning an encounter into something more like a transaction. One French couple I know that did meet on through an app have ended up married and with a baby. They were each other's first online date, and after meeting each other, they didn't try to date a multitude of other people too.

My current relationship is something of a case in point. Although my boyfriend was using dating apps, I was the first woman he ever met from one in real life. Perhaps this was because I approached it in a very different way, one that was more in line with my own culture. I sought to 'date' properly, meaning I made the effort to reply to his messages from the beginning. I have plenty of friends back home in the UK who met their spouses via sites like Match.com, Guardian Soulmates and Bumble, but I know very few in Paris. While I've had my own experiences, I wanted to ask my friend Elodie Fagan, senior marketing and communications manager for Tinder France, for some insights. She told me that, while French online dating behaviour is similar to other Western countries in some ways, the main difference is that they don't like to say what they're looking for. 'For example,' Elodie explains, 'we don't like to say we're looking for hook-ups. We don't like to give our intent. An overwhelming majority of French will say they're "looking for friends with romantic potential". In France, we're proud of our romantic nature and things happening by chance. We don't like to label things. And we're a lot more ambiguous when it comes to defining relationships.' She goes on to say, 'We approach love and dating in a very open-ended way: we don't know what we're looking for, we don't label relationships and we don't have the same dating "journey" as you do in the UK or the US.' My boyfriend shares this view.

In the Havas Group study I mentioned on page 314, they found that 70 per cent of French people trust the idea of finding love through random encounters. With this in mind, it makes sense that Happn, France's answer to Tinder and Bumble, uses 'hyper-location' technology to propose matches when users have crossed paths in real life. This approach harnesses the idea of 'happenstance' (coincidence) giving the illusion of 'a chance' encounter that's feels less transactional. Launched in 2014, Happn now has 77 million users worldwide, and its success is clearly linked to the app's attempt to 'reconcile the digital world with the physical one, using modern tools to capture some old-school magic'. It mirrors the way the French approach finding love in real life.

And although they're not necessarily big daters, I do think there's something that can be learned from their attitude towards it. When talking to my boyfriend about why he chose to put 'don't know what I'm looking for' on his Bumble profile instead of 'relationship' or 'something casual' (which are the other options), he said: 'How can I know what I'm looking for from someone until I've met them?' Whereas us Anglophones – me included, until I decided to practise a little more Parisienne in my approach to dating – have a tendency to define and force things too early, which can lead to more heartbreak and disappointments.

'Le Feeling'

A phrase that kept cropping up, time and time again, on many of the men's dating profiles I saw was simply two words: *'le feeling'*. It's a twist on the English word, and basically means a deeper connection that's more than just physical, or, as Magali Gnocchi puts it, *'le feeling* means the flow'. It's a fundamental ingredient for love, but one that can't always necessarily be explained, or put into words. *Le feeling* needs to be present in order for either party to want to pursue getting to know each other further. It can also be explained as something that isn't forced and, that feels natural and organic; it's essentially chemistry. It cannot be rationalised, but it's either there or it isn't.

Much can be learned from '*le feeling*' when it comes to dating and, ultimately, love. For example, I stayed in a relationship that was well past its sell-by date, thinking perhaps it might get better because of X, Y and Z: perhaps if we get married, that will give us a good project to work together towards. Or what if we have a baby? That might cement our love. Perhaps the problem is with the space we live in? All rather silly in hindsight, but how many of us have stayed in relationships (or 'situationships') because we thought we should? Ultimately, I was looking to outside things to try and change something inside – the way I felt about him. I was trying to rationalise my relationship by weighing up the reasons why I felt I should stay with him.

If only I had understood a little more about '*le feeling*', or had had the confidence to trust my gut and instincts. So, what can one learn from '*le feeling*'? Well, it can certainly help to explain why certain scenarios don't work out when dating. We've all heard the old saying 'he's just not that into you', but *le feeling* can help explain a deeper connection – or lack thereof – and help someone decide whether to commit to getting to know the other person better. *Le feeling* isn't personal, because it cannot be rationalised, and therefore it makes it easier to understand why the other party might not want to pursue a relationship. The dating scene is tough enough as it is. If you go into it armed with a little more know-how, a few more boundaries and fewer expectations, you'll be far better equipped to navigate the minefield of dating, rejections and uncertainty, ultimately helping you to find what you want – a great relationship.

What can we learn from the way Parisians date? To not put so much pressure or emphasis on the outcome; to go with the flow, to enjoy the journey and to not get too hung up on where it's going! A connection that leads to love should feel *effortless*. I've learned that it's important to know your values and to set boundaries, but beyond that you have to leave it to chance, having *le feeling* (or not) and chemistry. Someone could tick all your boxes, but perhaps you just don't have a connection. You cannot force it – so don't try to! In my experience, this doesn't work.

❧

Lessons I've learned in Paris about online dating

— When you're thinking about what to wear on
a first date, refer back to the chapters on style
and fashion and beauty, and opt for clothing and

make-up that make you feel comfortable, elegant and confident. Don't worry too much about trying to look sexy: as my Parisienne friends have taught me, that sexiness will come with being comfortable and confident in your own skin.

— Don't reply to a message immediately: leave it at least twenty minutes. Better yet, if he messages you in the morning, reply at lunch – let him know you're interested, but not too much. This also shows that you, of course, have your own life and are not waiting around for their message (even if you are!).

— Do not be the first one to send a message after the first date, or even the second. Let them do the work and they will if they're interested. If a guy likes you, he will find a way to message you and see you again. If you don't hear from him, it probably means that he's not that into you (no, he hasn't lost his phone or had it stolen). Leave it at least four days before contacting him, and even then, only do it because you need some closure – if you feel it will give you peace of mind and you have nothing to lose.

— Do not drink too much on a first date, but accept a second drink if you feel comfortable. A first date with someone you have met online can be a strange situation, and a glass of wine might help you feel more relaxed, but a first date isn't the time to overdo it on the alcohol.

— This might be a contentious one (and, for me, it applies only to a first date with someone you've met online), but allow the man to pay. You can offer, of course – it's polite – but let him pay if he offers. If he doesn't offer, it may be a sign that he is not very interested in you.

— This is more relevant if you live in Paris, but let him give you a ride home on his moped (scooter or *scoot* in French). If he has one and doesn't offer you a ride, take it that he's probably not that into you.

— Meeting someone online is very different to meeting someone in real life and then going on a 'date' together. Ideally, don't have sex on the first date of an online date if you're looking for a relationship. Get to know them a bit. The third date is the sweet spot. You can kiss on the second, and then have sex on the third or even fifth.

— Make lots of eye contact. It can speak volumes. Don't be afraid to pause and just meet his eyes for a minute. This can say a thousand words, and the silence creates a frisson of tension.

— Don't save a man's number in your phone until
they have earned their place in your address book.
I learned this from my friend Sutanya Dacres, who
I interview on page 336. It totally makes sense,
because it stops you getting too hung up on one
man too soon. At one point, during a brand dinner,
I had three different men messaging me and one
ringing me, and when my phone rang, I genuinely
didn't know which one it was. I have to admit,
I loved the sense of power it gave me.

— Do not air your dirty laundry on the first date.
Don't give too much away in the beginning. Of
course you should be yourself, but wait until you
have built a sense of closeness and intimacy with
someone before you start to share things that are
personal and private.

A conversation about love and dating in Paris with Sutanya Dacres

When writing this book and thinking about who I could interview about love and dating, Sutanya (@dinnerfor.one) immediately sprang to mind. Like me, Sutanya moved to Paris for love. She married a French man she met in a bar in New York and followed him to Paris. Sadly her marriage didn't last, and, like so many of us who follow our hearts to another country, she ended up single. The feelings of being alone and heartbroken are heightened by being in a foreign country, far from your friends and family. And yet, like so many others who have come to Paris for a love that didn't last, the experience has undoubtedly made her stronger. Sutanya had to walk her own path, confront life head-on, and, ultimately, make the most of it.

Like me, her experiences in Paris have shaped her and seen her grow into a woman she perhaps could never have become had she stayed in New York. She launched her own podcast, *Dinner For One*, as she wanted to share her perspective as a black American woman living in Paris, with a focus on how healing food can be. While cooking a meal in her Montmartre kitchen, she talks about love, dating and relationships in the City of Lights, as well as her passion for food and how cooking for herself (and others) has helped her through some of the darkest periods in her life. Sutanya is currently writing a book about her Parisian experience. I sat down with her to ask her a few questions about love.

What was it that attracted you to your French ex-husband?

I enjoyed his conversation. I found that, unlike the American men I was meeting at the time, he could have a conversation around something other than how much he had drunk the weekend before. He was interesting and seemed genuinely interested in me.

How do you think dating differs in Paris?

My answer to this could fill 500 pages and still need more! But, to keep it short, I think that the French throw themselves into a new relationship faster and with more intensity than Americans/Anglophones. Where Americans take our time to decide whether or not we want to be in a relationship with someone, the French seemingly decide before the end of date one, which leads to fleeting feelings and broken hearts. That was my experience.

What is different about the Parisian approach to love?

The French aren't afraid to fall in love. They're not afraid to put their hearts and emotions on the line, and if it doesn't work so be it. They're actually quite vulnerable in that way, and I admire that a lot. I also find French men overall a bit more direct. If they're really into you, you'll know.

What have you learned about love from living in Paris?

It's okay to have big feelings and express them. Love isn't something to be ashamed or scared of.

And what have you learned about dating and sex?

Dating is fun, but sex is even better.

What dating tips would you give to others?

I know this sounds clichéd, but really just be open to meeting different people – while also setting boundaries. If you think someone is taking you for a ride, put your foot down. Set expectations, and if you don't feel like you or your desires are being respected, then say '*Merci, mais non, au revoir*' and find someone that will respect you.

What tips would you give someone going through a break-up?

It's okay to feel sorry for yourself and be sad, but don't wallow in self-pity for too long, because it gets harder to pick yourself up. Never forget that there is a reason why your ex-partner was attracted to you and wanted to be with you in the first place, so in the end, although that person wasn't 'the one' for you, there is someone out there that will love – and put up with! – all parts of you.

What makes Paris so romantic?

I think it's the appreciation here for all things beautiful, the fact that people express that appreciation, and the intensity with which Parisians live their lives. Also, when you're surrounded by beauty, how can you not be romantic?

What have you learned about friendship from your time in Paris?

Friendships are just as important as intimate relationships. They've helped me grow and become the woman that I am today. From my French friends, in particular, I've learned that it's okay to be myself, flaws and all. Although I have flaws, they love me because of them, not despite them.

What are your favourite places to go in Paris?

Chez moi! No, but really, I am particularly biased towards the 18th arrondissement. I hesitate to name any specific place there, because shops and restaurants close and move, but if you're in Paris, I would recommend taking a stroll around the neighbourhood. Get off at metro Anvers and make your way all the way to Simplon. You'll see, feel and experience the charm of one of Paris's little villages.

A note on friendship

As anyone who has moved to a new country will know, whether you've moved for love, for a job or perhaps on a whim because you just wanted to experience living somewhere else, it's not always easy finding new friends. With no school or university structure creating ample social opportunities or acting as a cosy comforter in your quest for new friendships, making friends as an adult can be tough. Add a foreign language into the mix, and you don't have the best recipe for success.

When I said goodbye to my life in London, I also said goodbye to my closest friends. Of course there were text messages and phone calls, but nothing beats a real-life hug from a good friend. My friends have always been very important to me; I am an only child and think of my friends as family. I've always made friends pretty easily, perhaps because I'm happy to put in the effort, but making friends in a foreign country isn't the same experience. The goal posts are moved – rather dramatically. Fortunately, I was introduced to my first Parisian friend via an old colleague before I actually moved to Paris. We hit it off immediately (she'd lived in the US for a bit and spoke great English, so we didn't have a language barrier to contend with) and have stayed close ever since, even after her move to LA five years ago. But

I didn't make another close French friend until five years or so later.

It may be a stereotype, but there is some merit in it all the same: Parisians can be a little frosty. It's mainly because they're not used to inviting foreigners into their lives and homes in the same way we might do in cities like London, which is known to be a melting pot. I for one made lots of friends from different cultures and countries at university and throughout my twenties in London, but this isn't necessarily easy to do in Paris. It's a notion that was confirmed for me when I chatted to Philippine Darblay (see page 272). She lived in London for a number of years after studying for her Master's there, so, like me, she is able to make a good comparison between the two cities. She suggested that the Parisians can be a little more hesitant to make friends with outsiders, mainly because they're just not used to it. I would say, (in contrast to their Anglophone counterparts), Parisian women, for example are a little cooler upon first meeting: it takes them a while to thaw out. But once you peel back the layers, you'll find that you could have a friend for life, which has been my experience. This is perhaps because they tend to treat friendship a little differently here; they're not big on small talk and are not fans of 'surface' relationships. Of course, I'm generalising a little, but their friends are usually the same people they've known since they were at school, and they are less likely to make more *amis* (very close friends) during their adult lives. My Parisian boyfriend is testament to this.

Either way, I had to almost start from scratch. While I now have more French friends, it took a few years until my language level was good enough to converse and join in properly at social gatherings. In the beginning, like most expats, I migrated towards other expats. The 'expat' friendship is another breed of friendship entirely. You immediately have something in common in that you both moved to a different country, and, over the years, many of my expat friends have become like family. I was also fortunate enough to meet many of the friends I have today through Instagram back when it was more community-focused. I found a few like-minded souls and we began our friendships by meeting up in cafés around Paris. I've been lucky enough to build some really strong friendships since moving here, and I've learned a few things along the way.

Lessons I've learned about making friends as an adult

Find your tribe – It's important to befriend people that understand what makes you tick, but it's also important to have friends that support you through thick and thin – these are your tribe.

Look for like-minded souls – As I said earlier, Instagram was a huge help when it came to making friends, and I met many of my closest thanks to connecting via the app as I started following people who I felt had similar interests. If you do move to a new city, join clubs online and off – and follow people on Instagram. You never know, a contact could become a great connection.

Have friends for different things – Just as your boy-friend, husband or partner cannot give you everything you need, don't rely on one 'special' friend. You need a few. It's important to surround yourself with a supportive network of friends.

Put the effort in – Lasting friendship takes time and work! Just like any relationship, you have to put the effort in to reach out and stay in touch.

It should be give and take – Equally, a friendship should work both ways. If you find that you are doing all the work, perhaps it's time to re-evaluate the friendship. It shouldn't just be you making all the effort – you'd never want to be the person doing this in a romantic relationship.

Some friendships are not for ever – As with any rela-tionship, some friendships aren't meant to last forever. This is still one I find hard to reconcile with, but sadly it's true. Let friendships run their course. It's not worth trying to force a relationship or friendship that has fizzled out.

❧

A few of my favourite films set in or featuring Paris
French Kiss (1995)
Before Sunset (2004)
Amélie (2001)
Paris (2008)
La Boum (The Party) (1980)
Midnight in Paris (2011)
L'Arnacoeur (The Heartbreaker) (2010)
Les Intouchables (The Untouchables) (2011)
L'Homme Fidèle (A Faithful Man) (2018)
Je ne suis pas un homme facile (I'm Not an Easy Man)
    (2018)
Coco Before Chanel (2009)
Moulin Rouge! (2001)
Bande de Filles (Girlhood) (2018)
Sabrina (1954)
La Vie en Rose (2007)
Funny Face (1957)
Julie & Julia (2009)
Something's Gotta Give (2003)
Paris je t'aime (Paris, I Love You) (2006)
Santa & Cie (Christmas & Co.) (2017)

Epilogue: La vie en rose

26 April 2021

The process of writing this book and exploring everything that I've experienced and learned since moving to Paris has been as eye-opening, challenging and rewarding as living here for nearly a decade has. I'll admit there were times when I doubted myself, a little like when I first moved to the French capital and got cold feet. It's been an ambitious project, to say the least, to tackle the world's most written about city and people through five big subjects, adding my voice to an already crowded arena. Not to mention writing it during the coronavirus pandemic, one of the most unsettling and precarious periods of our times. It's been strange to write a book about all the aspects of Parisian life and culture that I love at a time when many of these wonderful things – dining in *caves á manger*, strolling in the streets, visiting museums and gathering with friends for an *apéro* – are off limits. But this time spent focusing on and writing about practising *Parisienne*, and thinking about life in this magnificent city – what I've learned from my fellow Parisians, how it has enhanced my life and how it could improve yours – has reaffirmed my *raison d'être* in more ways than one, and is also what helped get me through a very difficult year.

Committing to paper the lessons I've learned has also been an exercise in curation, a theme that has come up over and over again in this book as part of the Parisian approach to life. I could have easily kept on writing, packing in more lessons, advice and interviews, until I'd eventually written a whole book's worth of material for each chapter! But I had to stop at some point, reel myself in, refine my ideas, and focus on the facets that I thought you would find the most useful and inspiring. In doing so, I have curated my own capsule collection (or wardrobe, if you will) of the best Parisian tips for living. While I have tried to steer clear of the obvious Parisian clichés, some do, of course, actually ring true. Hopefully, though, what you will take away from this book are ideas to inspire you to live a little more *effortlessly* and better, as well as tips that you can integrate into your daily life that might raise your confidence, happiness and overall wellbeing levels a few bars.

As for me, despite some of the challenges and hardships I've faced while building a life for myself in this beautiful city, it has undoubtedly been the best experience I could have asked for – as has writing this book. So thank *you* for picking it up! As Edith Piaf once sang: *Non, je ne regrette rien.*

References and further reading

Fashion & Style

Alice Newbold, 'Hailey Beber, Lily Colins and Rosé are all obsessed with these French-girl bike shorts', vogue.co.uk, 16 December 2020.

Maude Bass-Kreuger, 'Everything to know about the history of the blazer', vogue.com.au, 28 November 2019.

'Le Smoking', Wikipedia (https://en.wikipedia.org/wiki/Le_Smoking).

Amy de Klerk, 'The history of the hero: the white shirt', harpersbazaar.com, 2020.

'The white shirt', tijdelijkmodemuseum. hetnieuweinstituut.nl/en/white-shirt.

Hayley Phelan, 'The straw bag: an obsessive, comprehensive guide', wsj.com, 6 July 2017.

'Dannijo Loves: straw bags', dannijo.com, 3 August 2019.

Jessica Michault 'Adding a splash of luxury to swimwear', nytimes.com, 8 August 2011.

Marlen Komar, 'The feminist history of the cardigan', theweek.com, 29 November 2019.

Anne-Sophie Mallard, 'Meet jewelry designer Anissa Kermiche', vogue.fr, 17 November 2016.

Beauty, skincare, body image & wellbeing

India Knight, 'His and hers: Borrow the boys' skincare heroes that work just as well on women.' *Sunday Times Style*, 11 August 2019.

Veronica McCarthy, 'La Bouche Rouge', wearedore.com.

Ariana Ionescu, 'What's French for bikini wax? A guide to grooming like a Parisian', vogue.com, 3 March 2018.

Deanna Pai, 'How spending a month in Paris made me way less self-conscious about body hair', glamour.com, 20 June 2016.

Sara Lieberman, 'How getting a bikini wax in Paris is helping me perfect my French', allure.com, 9 January 2018.

Charlotte Edwardes, 'Cleavage? Mais non!', thetimes.co.uk, 7 January 2017.

Morwenna Ferrier, 'The real reason French women have stopped sunbathing topless', theguardian.com, 28 July 2014.

Elian Peltier, 'Bare breasts on French beaches? You can, despite police warnings', newyorktimes.com, 26 August 2020.

Lauren Valenti, 'The #FreeTheNipple movement came Stateside in 2017 – but French girls have been doing it for decades', vogue.com, 27 December 2017.

Kerry Pieri, 'But will we ever wear bras again?', harpersbazaar.com, 8 April 2020.

Jessica Michault 'Adding a splash of luxury to
swimwear', nytimes.com, 8 August 2011.

Evelyn Lok, 'The wait is over: Celebrated perfume
house Goutal Paris lands in Hong Kong',
lifestyleasia.com, 8 October 2019.

Interiors & home life

Elizabeth Pash, 'What to look for when shopping
for Louis Philippe mirrors', housebeautiful.com,
10 May 2019.

Elise Taylor, 'Interior design trends to know in 2021
– and what's on its way out', vogue.com, 8 January
2021

Kate Arends, 'How to seek out unique second-hand
pieces online', witanddelight.com, 14 December
2020.

Dining out, drinking & café life

'Glossary of wine terms', winemag.com.

'60 useful French wine terms and expressions',
frenchtoday.com, 25 February 2021.

'A guide to the Sancerre region', vivino.com.

'Marché Dejean: Bienvenue dan le plus grande marché
Africain de Paris', portailafrique.fr.

'Made in Goutte d'Or', exploreparis.com.

'What is the difference between Pouilly-Fumé and
Pouilly-Fuissé?', winetime.com, 24 February 2019.

parisbymouth.com.

Relationships, love & dating

Aida Edemariam, 'Wild, controversial and free: Colette, a life too big for film', theguardian.com, 7 January 2019.

Alexandra Wolfe, 'Sophie Fontanel on "Sleeping Alone"', wsj.com, 16 August 2013.

'Happn CEO Didier Rapport is brining digital dating to life', europeanceo.com, 7 March 2019.

Constance Daire, 'Happn, le nouvel art de la drague à la française', capital.fr, 29 May 2020.

Anna Johnson, 'No sex please, we're married', theguardian.com, 6 January 2007.

Larry Getlen, 'The fascinating history of how courtship became dating', *New York Post*, 15 May 2016.

Lauren Collins, 'Dr Esther', newyorker.com, 24 July 2006.

Susan Dominus, 'The sexual healer', nytimes.com 24 January 2014.

'A Kiss is Just a Kiss' (episode 4, season 1), *Emily in Paris*, directed by Zoe Cassavetes, written by Darren Star, Kayla Alpert, Mat Whitaker, Jen Regan, Sarah Choi and Deborah Copaken.

Erica Schwiegershausen, 'Q&A: The fashion editor who resisted sex for 12 years', thecut.com, 7 August 2013.

Sophie Fontanel, 'Life without sex', nytimes.com, 20 July 2013.

Sara Roebuck, 'The things I learned from French women in Paris', medium.com, 7 July 2017.

Camille Chevalier-Karfis, 'French women don't date: the French dating system explained', frenchtoday. com, 9 February 2021.

James Wolcott, 'Liberté, fraternité, superiorité', vanityfair.com, 7 June 2013.

Hanna Rosin, 'No sex please, we're French', slate.com, 9 August 2013.

Debra Ollivier, 'The French philosophy on love and sex', huffpost.com, 15 May 2012.

Books and further reading

Deborah Ollivier, *What French Women Know: About Love, Sex, and Other Matters of Heart and Mind*, Piatkus, 2010.

David Lebovitz, *My Paris Kitchen: Recipes and Stories*, Ten Speed Press, 2014.

David Lebovitz, *L'Appart: The Delights and Disasters of Making My Paris Home*, Ballantine Books, 2018.

Sophie Mas, Audrey Diwan, Caroline de Maigret and Anne Berest, *How to be Parisian Wherever You Are*, Ebury, 2014.

Caroline de Maigret and Sophie Mas, *Older but Better, But Older: The Art of Growing Up*, Ebury, 2020.

References

Lindsey Tramuta, *The New Paris: The People, Places & Ideas Fuelling a Movement*, Abrams, 2017.

Garance Doré, *Love Style Life*, Simon & Schuster, 2015.

Jean-Benoit Nadeau and Julie Barlow, *Sixty Million Frenchmen Can't Be Wrong: What makes the French so French?* Robson, 2004.

Jeanne Damas and Lauren Bastide, *In Paris: 20 Women on Life in the City of Light*, Viking, 2018.

Inès de La Fressange and Sophie Gachet, *Parisian Chic Encore: A Style Guide*, Flammarion, 2019.

Inès de La Fressange and Marin Montagut, *Maison: Parisian Chic at Home*, Flammarion, 2018.

Vanessa Grall, *Don't be a Tourist in Paris*, Roads Publishing, 2017.

Rosa Park and Rich Stapleton, *Cereal City Guide: Paris*, Abrams, 2018.

Lauren Collins, *When in French: Love in a Second Language*, Penguin, 2017.

Stefania Rouselle, *Amour: How the French Talk about Love*, Viking, 2020.

Acknowledgements

And now, finally, to the thank yous and *merci beaucoups*!

Firstly, to my agent, Valeria Huerta, for believing in my book idea. Thank you also to Cyan Turan, for helping me turn the idea into a real proposal; to my commissioning editor, Anna Steadman, for taking a punt on me and buying my book; to Kate Miles, for your support and reassuring words during its writing; and to Tara O'Sullivan, for your excellent editing skills, and for reining me in where I had a tendency to repeat myself and waffle on. Thank you to Ruth Craddock for the beautiful illustrations; Heather Gatley for the cover illustrations; Sophie Ellis for the cover design and publicist Jessica Farrugia Sharples for your enthusiasm!

Thank you to everyone who has let me interview them or graciously contributed their ideas and words: without you, this book wouldn't be what it is. In the order they appear in the book, a huge thank you and *merci beaucoup* to: Vanessa Grall, Samar Seraqui de Buttafoco, Chrysoline de Gastines, Deborah Reyner Sebag, Anne-Laure Mais, Ellie Delphine, Monica de La Villardière, Marie Cilliot, Dr Oren Marco, Juliette Levy, Emma Hoareau, Laurie Zanoletti, Julie Pujols Benoit, Caroline Perrineau, Melanie Huynh, Sofiia Manousha, Jackie Kai Ellis, Géraldine Boublil, Charlotte Cadé,

Clémentine Lévy, Thibault Charpentier, Sarah Poniatowski, Eugénie Trochu, Rebekah Peppler, Philippine Darblay, Joann Pai, Frank Barron, Yasmin Zeinab, Fanny Flory, Elodie Fagan, Magali Gnocchi, Sophie Trem and Sutanya Dacres.

Thank you to my parents, who don't always agree with or understand my life choices, but love me unconditionally anyway: especially to my mum, for her unwavering support. Thanks also to my friends and family, but especially Pammy, Mariana, Lotts, Rachelle, Helen, Julia, Laura, Alicia and Sophie, who believe in me and champion me when I need it most – and, of course, to the friends I've made in Paris (you know who you are).

And to Victor, my Parisian, who met me (perhaps not so fortuitously for him, but certainly for me) during the writing of this book: who puts up with my bad French, English cooking and what I like to call 'crazies'; who welcomed me into his family, perhaps earlier than usual, when I couldn't see my own; and who has cheered me on throughout this writing journey. *Je t'aime.*

Index

Index

Index